MOORE'S

IRISH MELODIES

WITH

Symphonies and Accompaniments

BY

SIR JOHN STEVENSON, Mus. Doc.

AND

SIR HENRY BISHOP.

This edition was published in 1981
by Michael Glazier, Inc.
1210 King Street
Wilmington Delaware 19801

and

Gilbert Dalton Ltd.
4 Dublin Road
Stillorgan
County Dublin, Ireland

Library of Congress Catalog Card Number: 81-81465

International Standard Book Numbers:
    (Michael Glazier, Inc.): 0-89453-259-6
    (Gilbert Dalton Ltd.): 0-86233-026-2

Reprinted from the 1891 edition published by M. H. Gill & Son, Dublin.

Printed in the United States of America

MOORE'S
IRISH MELODIES.

WITH

Symphonies and Accompaniments

BY

SIR JOHN STEVENSON, Mus. Doc.

AND

SIR HENRY BISHOP.

New Edition

Michael Glazier, Inc.
Wilmington, Delaware

This Edition is Dedicated

to

John Caball

of

Tralee, County Kerry, Ireland.

CONTENTS.

MOORE'S
IRISH MELODIES.

FLY NOT YET.

AIR—PLANXTY KELLY.

Fly not yet, 'tis just the hour When

plea - sure, like the mid - night flow'r, That scorns the eye of vul - gar light, Be-

FLY NOT YET.

Joy so sel - dom weaves a chain Like this to - night, that, oh! 't is pain To

break its links so soon.

lentando.

II.

Fly not yet; the fount that play'd
In times of old through Ammon's shade,*
Though icy cold by day it ran,
Yet still, like souls of mirth, began
    To burn when night was near.
And thus should woman's heart and looks
At noon be cold as winter brooks,
Nor kindle till the night, returning,
Brings their genial hour for burning.
    Oh! stay,—oh! stay,—
When did morning ever break,
And find such beaming eyes awake
    As those that sparkle here?

* Solis Fons, near the Temple of Ammon.

WAR SONG.

REMEMBER THE GLORIES OF BRIEN THE BRAVE.

AIR—MOLLY MACALPIN.

* Brien Borombe, the great Monarch of Ireland, who was killed at the battle of Clontarf, in the beginning of the 11th century, after having defeated the Danes in twenty-five engagements. ** Munster. *** The Palace of Brien.

espress. lentando.

of-ten has pour'd Its beam on the battle, is set; But e-nough of its glo-ry re-

a tempo.

mains on each sword To light us to vic-to-ry yet!

II.

Mononia! when Nature embellish'd the tint
    Of thy fields, and thy mountains so fair,
Did she ever intend that a tyrant should print
    The footstep of slavery there?
No, Freedom, whose smile we shall never resign,
    Go, tell our invaders, the Danes,
That 't is sweeter to bleed for an age at thy shrine
    Than to sleep but a moment in chains!

III.

Forget not our wounded companions,* who stood
    In the day of distress by our side;
While the moss of the valley grew red with their blood,
    They stirr'd not, but conquer'd and died!
The sun, that now blesses our arms with his light,
    Saw them fall upon Ossory's plain:—
Oh! let him not blush, when he leaves us to-night,
    To find that they fell there in vain!

    * This alludes to an interesting circumstance related of the Dal gais, the favourite troops of Brien, when they were interrupted, in their return from the battle of Clontarf, by Fitzpatrick, Prince of Ossory. The wounded men entreated that they might be allowed to fight with the rest. "*Let stakes,*" they said, "*be stuck in the ground; and suffer each of us, tied to and supported by one of these stakes, to be placed in his rank by the side of a sound man.*"— "Between seven and eight hundred wounded men," adds O'Halloren, "pale, emaciated, and supported in this manner, appeared mixed with the foremost of the troops!— Never was such another sight exhibited." — HISTORY OF IRELAND, Book XII. Chap. I.

ERIN, THE TEAR AND THE SMILE IN THINE EYES.

AIR—AILEEN AROON.

E - rin, the tear and the smile in thine eyes Blend like the rain - bow that hangs in the skies; Shin-ing through sor - row's stream, Sadd'ning through pleasure's beam, Thy suns, with doubtful gleam, Weep while they rise!

II.

Erin! thy silent tear never shall cease,
Erin! thy languid smile ne'er shall increase,
Till, like the rainbow's light,
Thy various tints unite,
And form in Heaven's sight
One arch of peace!

HOW OFT HAS THE BENSHEE CRIED.

Slow, and with solemnity.

AIR—THE DEAR BLACK MAID.

How oft has the Ben-shee cried!

How oft has Death un-tied Bright links that Glo - ry wove, Sweet bonds en - twined by love!

Peace to each man - ly soul that slee-peth! Rest to each faith-ful eye that weepeth!

Long may the fair and brave Sigh o'er the he - ro's grave.

II.

We're fall'n upon gloomy days;
Star after star decays:
Ev'ry bright name, that shed
Light o'er the land, is fled.
Dark falls the tear of him who mourneth
Lost joy or hope, that ne'er returneth;
But brightly flows the tear
Wept o'er the hero's bier!

III.

Oh! quench'd are our beacon-lights,
Thou, of the hundred fights!
Thou, on whose burning tongue
Truth, peace, and freedom, hung!
Both mute—but, long as Valour shineth,
Or Mercy's soul at war repineth,
So long shall Erin's pride
Tell how they lived and died!

'T IS THE LAST ROSE OF SUMMER.

AIR—GROVES OF BLARNEY.

Feelingly.

'T is the last rose of sum-mer, Left bloom-ing a - lone; All her love - ly com - pan-ions Are fad - ed and gone; No flower of her kin - dred, No rose - bud is nigh, To re-flect back her blushes Or give sigh for sigh.

2ND VERSE.

i 'll not leave thee, thou lone one, To pine on the stem; Since the love - ly are sleeping, Go, sleep thou with them; Thus kind - ly I scat - ter Thy leaves o'er the bed, Where thy mates of the gar - den Lie scent - less and dead.

So soon may *I* follow,   When friendships decay,   And from love's shining circle   The gems drop away!
When true hearts lie wither'd,   And fond ones are flown,   Oh! who would inhabit   This bleak world alone?

WHEN HE WHO ADORES THEE.*

Slow and with feeling

AIR—THE FOX'S SLEEP.

When he who a-dores thee has left but the name Of his fault and his sor-row be-hind, Oh! say, wilt thou weep when they dark-en the fame Of a life that for thee was re-sign'd? Yes,

* These words allude to a story in an old Irish manuscript, which is too long and too melancholy to be inserted here.

weep! and, how-e-ver my foes may condemn, Thy tears shall ef-face their de-

cree; For Heav'n can wit-ness, though guil-ty to them, I have

been but too faith-ful to thee!

With thee were the dreams of my earliest love,
Every thought of my reason was thine:—
In my last humble pray'r to the Spirit above,
Thy name shall be mingled with mine!
Oh! bless'd are the lovers and friends who shall live
The days of thy glory to see;
But the next dearest blessing that Heaven can give
Is the pride of thus dying for thee!

2

THOUGH THE LAST GLIMPSE OF ERIN.

AIR-COULIN.

Tho' the last glimpse of E - RIN with sor - row I see, Yet wher - ev - - - er thou art shall seem E - RIN to me; In ex - ile thy bo - som shall still be my

home,   And thine eyes   make my cli - mate wher - e - ver we roam.

II.

To the gloom of some desert, or cold rocky snore,
Where the eye of the stranger can haunt us no more,
I will fly with my Coulin, and think the rough wind
Less rude than the foes we leave frowning behind: —

III.

And I'll gaze on thy gold hair, as graceful it wreathes,
And hang o'er thy soft harp, as wildly it breathes;
Nor dread that the cold-hearted Saxon will tear
One chord from that harp, or one lock from that hair.*

---

* "In the twenty-eighth year of the reign of Henry VIII. an Act was made respecting the habits and dress in general of the Irish, whereby all persons were restrained from being shorn or shaven above the ears, or from wearing Glibbes, or *Coulins* (long locks), on their heads, or hair on the upper lip, called *Crommeal*. On this occasion a Song was written by one of our bards, in which an Irish virgin is made to give the preference to her dear *Coulin* (or the youth with the flowing locks), to all strangers (by which the English were meant), or those who wore their habits. Of this song the Air alone has reached us, and is universally admired." — WALKER'S HISTORICAL MEMOIRS OF IRISH BARDS, page 134. — Mr. WALKER informs us also, that about the same period there were some harsh measures taken against the Irish Minstrels.

GO WHERE GLORY WAITS THEE.

AIR-MAID OF THE VALLEY.

Go where glo - ry waits thee, But while Fame e - lates thee, Oh! still re - member me.

When the praise thou meet - est, To thine ear is sweet - est,

Oh! then re - mem - ber me. O - ther arms may press thee,

Dear-er friends ca-ress thee, All the joys that bless thee Sweet-er far may be;

lentando.

But when friends are near-est, And when joys are dear-est, Oh! then re-mem-ber

me.

II.

When at eve thou rovest
By the star thou lovest,
    Oh! then remember me.
Think, when home returning,
Bright we've seen it burning.
    Oh! thus remember me.
Oft as summer closes,
When thine eye reposes
On its lingering roses,
    Once so loved by thee,
Think of her who wove them,
Her who made thee love them,
    Oh! then remember me.

III.

When, around thee dying,
Autumn leaves are lying,
    Oh! then remember me.
And, at night, when gazing.
On the gay hearth blazing,
    O! still remember me.
Then, should music, stealing
All the soul of feeling,
To thy heart appealing,
    Draw one tear from thee;
Then let memory bring thee
Strains I used to sing thee, —
    Oh! then remember me.

OH! BREATHE NOT HIS NAME.

AIR—THE BROWN MAID.

Oh! breathe not his

name — let it sleep in the shade, Where cold and un - ho - nour'd his

re - lics are laid! Sad, si - lent, and dark, be the tears that we shed, As the

night-dew that falls on the grass o'er his head!

II.

But the night-dew that falls, though in silence it weeps,
Shall brighten with verdure the grave where he sleeps;
And the tear that we shed, though in secret it rolls,
Shall long keep his memory green in our souls.

THE HARP THAT ONCE THROUGH TARA'S HALLS.

Slow.

AIR—GRAMMACHREE.

The Harp that once, thro' Ta-ra's halls, The soul of Mu-sic shed, Now hangs as mute on Ta-ra's walls As if that soul were fled:— So sleeps the pride of for-mer days, So

glo - ry's thrill is o'er; And hearts, that once beat high for praise, Now

feel that pulse no more!

II.

No more to chiefs and ladies bright
   The harp of Tara swells:
The chord alone, that breaks at night,
   Its tale of ruin tells.
Thus Freedom now so seldom wakes,
   The only throb she gives
Is when some heart indignant breaks,
   To show that still she lives.

RICH AND RARE WERE THE GEMS SHE WORE.

Moderate time.

AIR—THE SUMMER IS COMING.

Rich and

rare were the gems she wore,* And a bright gold ring on her wand she

bore;   bore; But, oh! her beau - ty was far be - yond Her

* This Ballad is founded upon the following anecdote:—"The people were inspired with such a spirit of honour, virtue, and religion by the great example of BRIEN, and by his excellent administration, that, as a proof of it, we are informed, a young lady of great beauty, adorned with jewels and a costly dress, undertook a journey alone from one end of the kingdom to the other with a wand only in her hand, at the top of which was a ring of exceeding great value; and such an impression had the laws and government of this monarch made on the minds of all the people, that no attempt was made upon her honour, nor was she robbed of her clothes or jewels."
—WARNER'S HISTORY OF IRELAND, Vol. I. Book 10.

spark - ling   gems   and   snow - white   wand. But   oh!   her   beau - ty was

far   be - yond   Her   spark - ling   gems   and   snow - white   wand.

II.

"Lady, dost thou not fear to stray,
So lone and lovely, through this bleak way?
Are Erin's sons so good or so cold,
As not to be tempted by woman or gold?"

III.

"Sir Knight! I feel not the least alarm,
No son of Erin will offer me harm:
For, though they love women and golden store,
Sir Knight! they love honour and virtue more."

IV.

On she went, and her maiden smile
In safety lighted her round the green isle;
And blest for ever is she who relied
Upon Erin's honour and Erin's pride.

AS A BEAM O'ER THE FACE OF THE WATERS MAY GLOW.

Pensively.

AIR—THE YOUNG MAN'S DREAM.

As a beam o'er the face of the wa-ters may glow, While the tide runs in dark-ness and cold-ness be-low, So the cheek may be tinged with a warm sun-ny smile, Tho' the cold heart to ru-in runs dark-ly the while.

III.

Oh! this thougth in the midst of enjoyment will stay,
Like a dead leafless branch in the summer's bright ray;
The beams of the warm Sun play round it in vain —
It may smile in his light, but it blooms not again!

THE MEETING OF THE WATERS.*

AIR—THE OLD HEAD OF DENIS.

There is not in the wide world a val-ley so sweet As that

vale in whose bo-som the bright wa-ters meet.† Oh! the last rays of feel-ing and

* "The meeting of the Waters" forms a part of that beautiful scenery which lies between Rathdrum and Arklow, in the county of Wicklow; and these lines were suggested by a visit to this romantic spot in the summer of the year 1807.

† The rivers Avon and Avoca.

life must de - part Ere the bloom of that val - ley shall fade from my heart! Ere the

bloom of that val - ley shall fade from my heart!

II.

Yet is *was* not that Nature had shed o'er the scene
Her purest of crystal and brightest of green;
'Twas *not* her soft magic of streamlet or hill,
Oh! no—it was something more exquisite still.

III.

'Twas that friends, the beloved of my bosom, were near,
Who made every dear scene of enchantment more dear,
And who felt how the best charms of Nature improve,
When we see them reflected from looks that we love.

IV.

Sweet vale of Avoca! how calm could I rest
In thy bosom of shade, with the friends I love best,
Where the storms that we feel in this cold world should cease,
And our hearts, like thy waters, be mingled in peace.

ST. SENANUS AND THE LADY.

AIR—THE BROWN THORN.

"Oh! haste and leave this sa-cred isle, Un-ho-ly bark! ere morn-ing smile; For on thy deck, tho' dark it be, A fe-male form I see; And I have sworn this sainted

sod   Shall ne'er by wo - man's feet be trod.

2ND VERSE.

THE LADY.   "Oh! Fa - ther, send   not hence my bark, Thro' win - try

winds, and o'er bil - lows dark; I come, with hum - ble heart, to   share   Thy morn and

ev'n - ing pray'r; Nor mine the feet,   O ho - ly Saint,   The brightness

of   thy sod to   taint."

III. The Lady's prayer Senanus spurn'd; The wind blew fresh, and the bark return'd; But legends hint, that had the maid Till morning's light delay'd, And given the Saint one rosy smile, She ne'er had left his lonely isle.

HOW DEAR TO ME THE HOUR WHEN DAY-LIGHT DIES.

Slow, and to be played very smoothly.

AIR—THE TWISTING OF THE ROPE.*

How dear to me the hour when day - light dies, And sun - beams melt a - long the si - lent sea; For then sweet dreams of o - ther days a - rise, And Mem' - ry breathes her ves - per sigh to thee! For

then sweet dreams of o-ther days a-rise, And Mem'ry breathes her ves-per

sigh to thee!

II.

And, as I watch the line of light that plays
Along the smooth wave t'ward the burning west,
I long to tread that golden path of rays,
And think 'twould lead to some bright isle of rest.

TAKE BACK THE VIRGIN PAGE.*

AIR—DERMOTT.

With feeling.

Take back the vir - gin page, White and un - writ - ten still;

Some hand, more calm and sage, The leaf must fill. Thoughts come as pure as light,

Pure as ev'n you re - quire; But oh! each word I write Love turns to fire. fire.

* Written on returning a blank book.

2ND VERSE.

Yet let me keep the book; Oft shall my heart re-new,

lentando.

When on its leaves I look, Dear thoughts of you! Like you 'tis fair and bright;

lentando.　1st.　2nd.

Like you, too bright and fair To let wild Passion write One wrong wish there! there.

mf lento.

III. Haply, when from those eyes Far, far away I roam, Should calmer thoughts arise Tow'rds you and home,
Fancy may trace some line Worthy those eyes to meet; Thoughts that not burn, but shine, Pure, calm,
and sweet!

IV. And, as the records are, Which wand'ring seamen keep, Led by their hidden star Through winter's deep;
So may the words I write Tell through what storms I stray, *You* still the unseen light, Guiding my way!

THE LEGACY.

WHEN IN DEATH I SHALL CALM RECLINE.

With Feeling and Gaiety.

AIR—UNKNOWN.

When in death I shall calm re - cline, O bear my heart to my mis-tress dear; Tell her it lived up - on smiles, and wine Of the bright - est hue, while it lin - ger'd here: Bid her not shed one tear of sor - row To sul - ly a heart so

brilliant and light; But bal - my drops from the red grape bor-row, To bathe the re - lic from

morn till night.

II.

When the light of my song is o'er,
    Then take my harp to your ancient hall
Hang it up at that friendly door,
    Where weary travellers love to call.*
Then if some bard, who roams forsaken,
    Revive its soft note in passing along,
Oh! let one thought of its master waken
    Your warmest smile for the child of song.

III.

Keep this cup, which is now o'erflowing
    To grace your revel when I'm at rest;
Never, oh! never its balm bestowing
    On lips that beauty hath seldom bless'd.
But when some warm devoted lover
    To her he adores shall bathe its brim,
Then, then my spirit around shall hover,
    And hallow each drop that foams for him.

* "In every house was one or two Harps, free to all travellers, who were the more caressed, the more they excelled in Music." — O'HALLORAN.

WE MAY ROAM THROUGH THIS WORLD.

Merrily.

AIR—GARYYONE.

We may roam thro' this world like a child at a feast, Who but sips of a sweet, and then flies to the rest, And, when pleasure be-gins to grow dull in the east, We may or-der our wings and be off to the west; But if hearts that feel, and eyes that smile, Are the dear-est gifts that Heav'n supplies, We nev-er need leave our own Green Isle For sen-si-tive hearts and for

sun-bright eyes. Then re - mem-ber, wher-ev - er your gob - let is crown'd, Thro' this world whether

east-ward or westward you roam, When a cup to the smile of dear wo - man goes round, Oh! re-

mem-ber the smile which a-dorns her at home.

II.

In England the garden of Beauty is kept
  By a dragon of prudery, placed within call;
But so oft this unamiable dragon has slept,
  That the garden's but carelessly watch'd, after all.
Oh! they want the wild sweet-briery fence,
  Which round the flow'rs of Erin dwells,
Which warns the touch while winning the sense,
  Nor charms us least when it most repels.
Then remember, wherever your goblet is crown'd,
  Thro' this world whether eastward or westward you
                    roam,
When a cup to the smile of dear woman goes round,
  Oh! remember the smile which adorns her at home.

III.

In France, when the heart of a woman sets sail,
  On the ocean of wedlock its fortune to try,
Love seldom goes far in a vessel so frail,
  But just pilots her off, and then bids her good-bye!
While the daughters of Erin keep the boy
  Ever smiling beside his faithful oar,
Thro' billows of woe and beams of joy,
  The same as he look'd when he left the shore.
Then remember, wherever your goblet is crown'd,
  Thro' this world whether eastward or westward you
                    roam,
When a cup to the smile of dear woman goes round,
  Oh! remember the smile which adorns her at home.

EVELEEN'S BOWER.

AIR—UNKNOWN.

Oh! weep for the hour, When to E-ve-leen's bower The Lord of the Val-ley with

false vows came; The moon hid her light From the Heavens that night, And wept be-hind her

clouds o'er the mai-den's shame. The clouds past soon From the chaste cold moon, And

Heav'n smiled a-gain with her ves-tal flame; But none will see the day When the

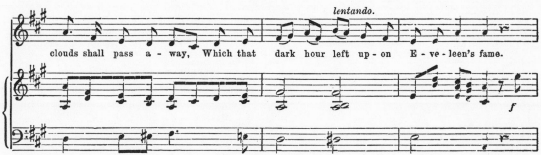

lentando.

clouds shall pass a - way, Which that dark hour left up - on E - ve - leen's fame.

II.

The white snow lay
On the narrow pathway
When the Lord of the Valley cross'd over the moor;
And many a deep print
On the white snow's tint
Show'd the track of his footsteps to Eveleen's door.
The next sun's ray
Soon melted away
Every trace on the path where the false Lord came;
But there's a light above,
Which alone can remove
That stain upon the snow of fair Eveleen's fame.

LET ERIN REMEMBER THE DAYS OF OLD.

* "This brought on an encounter between Malachi (the Monarch of Ireland in the Tenth Century) and the Danes, in which Malachi defeated two of their Champions, whom he encountered successively hand to hand, taking a Collar of Gold from the neck of one, and carrying off the Sword of the other, as trophies of his victory." — WARNER'S HISTORY OF IRELAND, Vol. I. Book 9.

green un-furl'd, Led the Red-Branch Knights * to dan - ger, Ere the em' - rald gem of the

west - ern world Was set in the crown of a stran - ger.

On Lough-Neagh's bank, † as the fisherman strays,
When the clear cold eve's declining,
He sees the round towers of other days
In the wave beneath him shining!
Thus shall Memory often, in dreams sublime,
Catch a glimpse of the days that are over;
Thus, sighing, look through the waves of Time
For the long-faded glories they cover!

* "Military Orders of Knights were very early established in Ireland; long before the birth of CHRIST we find an hereditary Order of Chivalry in Ulster, called *Curaidhe na Craoibhe ruadh*, or the Knights of the Red Branch, from their chief seat in Emania, adjoining to the Palace of the Ulster Kings, called *Teagh na Craoibhe ruadh*, or the Academy of the Red Branch; and contiguous to which was a large Hospital, founded for the sick Knights and Soldiers, called *Bron-bhearg*, or the House of the Sorrowful Soldier."—O'HALLORAN'S INTRODUCTION, &c. Part I. Chap. 5.

† It was an old tradition, in the time of Giraldus, that Lough-Neagh had been originally a fountain, by whose sudden overflowing the country was inundated, and a whole region, like the Atlantis of Plato, overwhelmed. He says that the fishermen, in clear weather, used to point out to strangers the tall ecclesiastical towers under the water: — "*Piscatores aquæ illius turres ecclesiasticas, quæ more patriæ arctæ sunt et altæ, necnon et rotundæ, sub undis manifeste sereno tempore conspiciunt, et extraneis transeuntibus reique causas admirantibus frequenter ostendunt.*" — TOPOGR. HIB. DIST. 2, C. 9.

SILENT, O MOYLE! BE THE ROAR OF THY WATER.

THE SONG OF FIONNUALA.*

Mournfully.

AIR—ARRAH, MY DEAR EVELEEN.

Si - lent, O Moyle! be the roar of thy wa-ter, Break not, ye breez-es! your

chain of re - pose, While, mur - mur-ing mourn - ful-ly, Lir's lone-ly daughter

Tells to the night - star her tale of woes. When shall the Swan, her

* Tho make this story intelligible in a Song would require a much greater number of verses than any one is authorized to inflict upon an audience at once; the reader must therefore be content to learn, in a note, that Fionnuala, the daughter of Lir, was, by some supernatural power, transformed into a Swan, and condemned to wander, for many hundred years, over certain lakes and rivers of Ireland, till the coming of Christianity, when the first sound of the Mass-bell was to be the signal of her release. — I found this fanciful fiction among some manuscript translations from the Irish, which were begun under the direction of that enlightened friend of Ireland, the late Countess of MOIRA.

death-note sing-ing,   Sleep with wings in   dark - ness furl'd?   When will Heav'n, its

sweet   bell   ring-ing,   Call   my spi-rit from this   storm-y   world?

II.

Sadly, o Moyle! to thy winter-wave weeping,
  Fate bids me languish long ages away;
Yet still in her darkness doth Erin lie sleeping,
  Still doth the pure light its dawning delay!
When will that day-star, mildly springing,
  Warm our Isle with peace and love?
When will Heaven, its sweet bell ringing,
  Call my spirit to the fields above?

COME, SEND ROUND THE WINE.

Spirited.

AIR—WE BROUGHT THE SUMMER WITH US.

Come, send round the wine, and leave points of be - lief To sim - ple - ton sa - ges and

reas'n - ing fools; This mo - ment's a flow'r too fair and brief, To be wi - ther'd and stain'd by the

dust of the schools, Your glass may be pur - ple and mine may be blue; But

while they're both fill'd from the same bright bowl, The fool that would quar-rel for

diff - rence of hue De - serves not the com - fort they shed o'er the soul.

II.

Shall I ask the brave soldier who fights by my side
In the cause of mankind, if our creeds agree?
Shall I give up the friend I have valued and tried,
If he kneel not before the same altar with me?
From the heretic girl of my soul should I fly,
To seek somewhere else a more orthodox kiss?
No, perish the hearts, and the laws that try
Truth, valour, or love, by a standard like this!

SUBLIME WAS THE WARNING WHICH LIBERTY SPOKE.

With spirit.

AIR--THE BLACK JOKE.

Sub - lime was the warn-ing which Li - ber - ty spoke, And grand was the mo - ment when

Spaniards a - woke In - to life and re - venge from the Con-quer-or's chain!

Oh, Li - ber - ty! let not this spi - rit have rest Till it move, like a breeze, o'er the

waves of the west— Give the light of your look to each sor - row - ing spot, Nor,

oh! be the Sham-rock of E-rin for-got While you add to your gar-land the

Ol-ive of Spain!

II.

If the fame of our fathers, bequeath'd with their rights,
Give to country its charm and to home its delights;
 If deceit be a woand and suspicion a stain;
Then, ye men of Iberia! our cause is the same —
And, oh! may his tomb want a tear and a name,
Who would ask for a nobler, a holier death,
Than to turn his last sigh into Victory's breath
 For the Shamrock of Erin and Olive of Spain!

III.

Ye Blakes and O'Donnels, whose fathers resign'd
The green hills of their youth, among strangers to find
 That repose which, at home, they had sigh'd for in vain,
Breathe a hope that the magical flame, which you light,
May be felt yet in Erin, as calm and as bright;
And forgive even Albion, while, blushing, she draws,
Like a truant, her sword, in the long-slighted cause
 Of the Shamrock of Erin and Olive of Spain!

IV.

God prosper the cause! — Oh! it cannot but thrive,
While the pulse of one patriot heart is alive,
 Its devotion to feel and its rights to maintain:
Then how sainted by sorrow its martyrs will die!
The finger of glory shall point where they lie;
While far from the footstep of coward or slave,
The young Spirit of Freedom shall shelter their grave
 Beneath Shamrocks of Erin and Olives of Spain!

BELIEVE ME, IF ALL THOSE ENDEARING YOUNG CHARMS.

With feeling.

AIR—MY LODGING IS ON THE COLD GROUND.

Be - lieve me, if all those en - dear - ing young charms, Which I gaze on so fond - ly to-

day, Were to change by to - mor-row, and fleet in my arms, Like fair-y gifts, fad - ing a-

way,— Thou wouldst still be a - dored as this mo - ment thou art, Let thy

love - li - ness fade as it will; And a - round the dear ru - in each

wish of my heart Would en - twine it - self ver - dant - ly still!

II.

It is not while beauty and youth are thine own,
And thy cheeks unprofaned by a tear,
That the fervour and faith of a soul can be known,
To which time will but make thee more dear;
No, the heart that has truly loved never forgets,
But as truly loves on to the close,
As the sun-flower turns on her god, when he sets,
The same look which she turn'd when he rose.

LIKE THE BRIGHT LAMP.

With feeling and solemnity.

AIR—THAMAMA HALLA.

Like the bright lamp that lay on Kil - dare's ho - ly shrine,* And burn'd thro' long a - ges of dark-ness and storm, Is the heart that sor - rows have frown'd on in vain, Whose spi - rit out - lives them, un - fad - ing and warm! E - rin! oh E - rin! thus bright, thro' the tears Of a long night of

* The inextinguishable fire of St. Bridget, at Kildare, which Giraldus mentions.

bond - age, thy spi - rit ap - pears! E - rin! oh E - rin! thus bright, thro' the

tears Of a long nigth of bond - age, thy spi - rit ap - pears.

II.

The nations have fallen, and thou still art young.
  Thy sun is but rising, when others are set:
And though slavery's cloud o'er thy morning hath hung
  The full noon of freedom shall beam round thee yet.
Erin, O Erin! though long in the shade,
Thy star will shine out when the proudest shall fade.

III.

Unchill'd by the rain, and unwaked by the wind,
  The lily lies sleeping through winter's cold hour,
Till Spring's light touch her fetters unbind,
  And daylight and liberty bless the young flow'r.
Thus Erin, O Erin! *thy* winter is past,
And the hope that lived through it shall blossom at last.

56

OH! THINK NOT MY SPIRITS ARE ALWAYS AS LIGHT.

AIR—JOHN O'REILLY THE ACTIVE.

Oh! think not my spir-its are al-ways as light And as free from a pang, as they

seem to you now; Nor ex-pect that the heart-beam-ing smile of to-night Will re-

ne-ver meet worse in our pil - grimage here Than the tear that en - joy-ment can

gild with a smile, And the smile that com - pas - sion can turn to a tear!

II.

The thread of our life would be dark, Heaven knows!
    If it were not with friendship and love intertwined;
And I care not how soon I may sink to repose,
    When these blessings shall cease to be dear to my mind.
But they who have loved the fondest, the purest,
    Too often have wept o'er the dream they believed;
And the heart that has slumber'd in friendship securest
    Is happy indeed if 'twas never deceived.
But send round the bowl; while a relic of truth
    Is in man or in woman, this prayer shall be mine, —
That the sunshine of love may illumine our youth,
    And the moonlight of friendship console our decline.

THE ORIGIN OF THE HARP.

AIR—GAGE FANE.

'T is believed that this Harp, which I wake now for thee, Was a Sy-ren, of old, who sung under the

sea; And who often at eve through the bright bil-low roved, To meet on the green shore a

youth whom she loved.

II.

But she loved him in vain, for he left her to weep,
And in tears all the night, her gold tresses to steep,
Till Heaven look'd with pity on true love so warm,
And changed to this soft Harp the sea-maiden's form.

III.

Still her bosom rose fair—still her cheeks smiled the same—
While her sea-beauties gracefully form'd the light frame;
And her hair, as, let loose, o'er her white arm it fell,
Was changed to bright chords, uttering melody's spell.

IV.

Hence it came that this soft Harp so long hath been known
To mingle love's language with sorrow's sad tone;
Till *thou* didst divide them, and teach the fond lay,
To speak love when I'm near tnee, and grief when away!

DRINK TO HER.

Playful.

AIR—HEIGH HO! MY JACKEY.

Drink to her, who long Hath waked the po-et's sigh—The girl, who gave to Song What gold could nev-er buy! Oh! wo-man's heart was made For

minstrel-hands a-lone! By o-ther fing-ers play'd, It yields not half the tone. Then

here's to her who long Hath waked the po-et's sigh—The girl, who gave to Song What

gold could nev-er buy!

II.

At Beauty's door of glass
  When Wealth and Wit once stood,
They ask'd her, "which might pass?"
  She answer'd, "he who could."
With golden key Wealth thought
  To pass—but 'twould not do:
While Wit a diamond brought,
  Which cut his bright way through.
So here's to her who long
  Hath waked the poet's sigh,
The girl who gave to song
  What gold could never buy.

III.

The love that seeks a home
  Where wealth and grandeur shines,
Is like the gloomy gnome
  That dwells in dark gold mines.
But oh! the poet's love
  Can boast a brighter sphere;
Its native home's above,
  Though woman keeps it here.
Then drink to her who long
  Hath waked the poet's sigh,
The girl who gave to song
  What gold could never buy.

OH! BLAME NOT THE BARD.*

AIR—KITTY TYRREL.

With expression.

Oh! blame not the bard, if he fly to the bow'rs, Where pleasure lies, care-less-ly

smil-ing at fame; He was born for much more, and, in hap-pi-er hours, His

soul might have burn'd with a ho-li-er flame. The string, that now lan-guish-es

* We may suppose this apology to have been uttered by one of those wandering bards whom Spencer so severely, and, perhaps, truly describes in his state of Ireland, and whose poems, he tells us, "were sprinkled with some pretty flowers of their natural device, which gave good grace and comeliness unto them; the which it is great pity to see abused to the gracing of wickedness and vice, which, with good usage, would serve to adorn and beautify virtue."

loose o'er the lyre, Might have bent a proud bow * to the war - - ri-or's dart; And the

lip, which now breathes but the song of de-sire, Might have pour'd the full tide of the

pa - tri - ot's heart!

II.

But, alas for his country!—her pride has gone by,
And that spirit is broken, which never would bend;
O'er the ruin her children in secret must sigh,
For 'tis treason to love her, and death to defend.
Unprized are her sons, till they've learn'd to betray;
Undistinguish'd they live, if they shame not their sires;
And the torch, that would light them through dignity's way,
Must be caught from the pile where their country ex-
pires.

III.

Then blame not the bard, if in pleasure's soft dream
He should try to forget what he never can heal;
Oh! give but a hope—let a vista but gleam
Through the gloom of his country, and mark how he'll
feel!
That instant, his heart at her shrine would lay down;
Every passion it nursed, every bliss it adored.
While the myrtle, now idly entwined with his crown,
Like the wreath of Harmodious, should cover his sword.†

IV.

But though glory be gone, and though hope fade away,
Thy name, lovèd Erin, shall live in his songs;
Not even in the hour when his heart is most gay,
Will he lose the remembrance of thee and thy wrongs.
The stranger shall hear thy lament on his plains;
The sigh of thy harp shall be sent o'er the deep,
Till thy masters themselves, as they rivet thy chains,
Shall pause at the song of their captive, and weep!

* It is conjectured by Wormius, that the name of Ireland is derived from *Yr*, the Runic for a *bow*, in the use of which weapon the Irish were once very expert. This derivation is certainly more creditable to us than the following: — "So that Ireland, (called the land of *Ire*, for the constant broils therein for 400 years), was now become the land of concord." LLOYD's *State Worthies*. Art. 'The Lord Grandison.'
† See the Hymn attributed to Alcæus, Ἐν μυρτοί χλάδι τὸ ξίφος φορήρω — "I will carry my sword, hidden in myrtles, like Harmodius and Aristogiton," &c.

WHILE GAZING ON THE MOON'S LIGHT.

AIR-OONAGH.

While gaz-ing on the moon's light, A mo-ment from her smile I turn'd, To

look at orbs, that, more bright, In lone and dis-tant glo-ry burn'd: But too far Each

proud star For me to feel its warm-ing flame; Much more dear That mild sphere, Which

near our pla-net smil-ing came: Thus, Ma-ry dear! be thou my own—While bright-er eyes un-

heed-ed play, I'll love these moonlight looks a-lone, Which bless my home, and guide my way!

8va - - - - - - - - - -

II.

The day had sunk in dim showers,
   But midnight now, with lustre meek,
Illumined all the pale flowers,
   Like hope, that ligths a mourner's cheek.
     I said (while
     The moon's smile
   Play'd o'er a stream, in dimpling bliss),
     "The moon looks
     On many brooks;
   The brook can see no moon but this."
And thus, I thougth, our fortunes run,
   For many a lover looks to thee;
While, oh! I feel there is but *one*,
   One Mary in the world for me!

5

WHEN DAYLIGHT WAS YET SLEEPING.

ILL OMENS.

AIR—KITTY OF COLERAINE; OR, PADDY'S RESOURCE.

Moderate time.

When day - light was yet sleep - ing un - der the bil - low, And stars in the hea - vens still

lin - ger - ing shone, Young Kit - ty, all blushing, rose up from her pil - low, The

last time she e'er was to press it a - lone: For the youth, whom she treasured her

heart and her soul in, Had promised to link the last tie be - fore noon; And when

once the young heart of a maid-en is stol-en, The maid-en her-self will steal

af - ter it soon!

II.

As she look'd in the glass, which a woman ne'er misses,
  Nor ever wants time for a sly glance or two,
A butterfly, fresh from the night-flower's kisses,
  Flew over the mirror, and shaded her view.
Enraged with the insect for hiding her graces,
  She brush'd him — he fell, alas! — never to rise: —
"Ah! such," said the girl, "is the pride of our faces,
  For which the soul's innocence too often dies!"

III.

While she stole through the garden, where heart's-ease was growing,
  She cull'd some, and kiss'd off its night-fallen dew;
And a rose, further on, look'd so tempting and glowing,
  That, spite of her haste, she must gather it too:
But, while o'er the roses too carelessly leaning,
  Her zone flew in two, and the heart's-ease was lost: —
"Ah! this means," said the girl, (and she sigh'd at its meaning,)
  "That love is scarce worth the repose it will cost!"

BEFORE THE BATTLE.

BY THE HOPE WITHIN US SPRINGING.

AIR—THE FAIRY QUEEN.
Harmonized for four voices.

OH! THE DAYS ARE GONE, WHEN BEAUTY BRIGHT.

Moderate time, with expression.

AIR—THE OLD WOMAN.

Oh! the days are gone, when beau-ty bright My heart's chain wove, When my

dream of life from morn 'till night, Was love, still love! New hope may bloom And

days may come, Of mild-er, calm-er beam, But there's nothing half so sweet in life As

II.

Oh! that fairy form is ne'er forgot,

Which first love traced;

Still it ling'ring haunts the greenest spot

On mem'ry's waste!

'T was odour fled

As soon as shed;

'T was morning's winged dream!

'T was a light, that ne'er can shine again

On life's dull stream!

Oh! 't was light, that ne'er can shine again

On life's dull stream!

NIGHT CLOSED AROUND THE CONQUEROR'S WAY.

(AFTER THE BATTLE.)

With solemnity.

AIR—THY FAIR BOSOM.

Night closed a - round the conqueror's way, And lightning show'd the dis - tant hill, Where

those, who lost that dread-ful day, Stood few and faint, but fear-less still! The soldier's

II.

The last sad hour of Freedom's dream
    And Valour's task moved slowly by,
While mute they watch'd, till morning's beam
    Should rise, and give them light to die! —
There is a world, where souls are free,
    Where tyrants taint not Nature's bliss:|
If death that world's bright opening be,
    Oh! who would live a slave in this?

OH! 'T IS SWEET TO THINK.

AIR—THADY, YOU GANDER.

Oh! 'tis sweet to think that, where'er we rove, We are sure to find something blissful and dear, And that,

when we're far from the lips we love, We have but to make love to the lips we are near! The

heart, like a ten-dril, ac-cus-tom'd to cling, Let it grow where it will, can-not flour-ish a-lone, But will

lean to the near-est and love-li-est thing It can twine with it-self, and make

II.

'T were a shame, when flowers around us rise,
   To make light of the rest if the rose is not there;
And the world's so rich in resplendent eyes,
   'T were a pity to limit one's love to a pair.
Love's wing and the peacock's are nearly alike;
   They are both of them bright, but they're changeable too:
And, wherever a new beam of beauty can strike,
   It will tincture Love's plume with a different hue.
Then, oh! what pleasure, where'er we rove,
   To be doom'd to find something still that is dear;
And to know, when far from the lips we love,
   We have but to make love to the lips we are near!

THROUGH GRIEF AND THROUGH DANGER.

(THE IRISH PEASANT TO HIS MISTRESS.)

With feeling.

AIR—I ONCE HAD A TRUE LOVE.

Thro' grief and thro' dan-ger thy smile hath cheer'd my way, Till
hope seem'd to bud from each thorn, that round me lay; The dark - er our for - tune, the
bright - er our pure love burn'd, Till shame in - to glo - ry, till fear in - to zeal was

turn'd; Oh! slave as I was, in thy arms my spir-it felt free, And bless'd ev'n the

sor - rows that made me more dear to thee.

II.

Thy rival was honour'd, whilst thou wert wrong'd and scorn'd,
Thy crown was of briers, while gold her brows adorn'd;
She woo'd me to temples, while thou layest hid in caves,
Her friends were all masters, while thine, alas! were slaves;
Yet cold in the earth, at thy feet, I would rather be,
Than wed what I love not, or turn one thought from thee.

III.

They slander thee sorely, who say thy vows are frail —
Hadst thou been a false one, thy cheek had look'd less pale.
They say too, so long thou hast worn those lingering chains,
That deep in thy heart they have printed their servile stains —
Oh! foul is the slander — no chain could that soul subdue —
Where shineth *thy* spirit, there liberty shineth too!

ON MUSIC.

WHEN THROUGH LIFE UNBLEST WE ROVE.

AIR—BANKS OF BANNA.

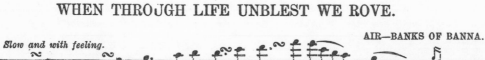

When thro' life un-blest we rove, Los-ing all that made life dear,

Should some notes, we used to love In days of boy - hood, meet our ear;

Oh! how wel - come breathes the strain, Wak'ning thoughts that long have slept —

Kind - ling form - er smiles a - gain In fad - ed eyes, that long have wept!

II.

Like the gale that sighs along
    Beds of oriental flowers,
Is the grateful breath of song
    That once was heard in happier hours;
Fill'd with balm, the gale sighs on,
    Though the flowers have sunk in death;
So, when pleasure's dream is gone,
    Its memory lives in Music's breath.

III.

Music! oh, how faint, how weak,
    Language fades before thy spell!
Why should Feeling ever speak,
    When thou canst breathe her soul so well?
Friendship's balmy words may feign,
    Love's are even more false than they;
Oh! 't is only Music's strain
    Can sweetly soothe, and not betray!

IT IS NOT THE TEAR AT THIS MOMENT SHED.*

With expression.

AIR—THE SIXPENCE.

It is not the tear at this mo-ment shed, When the cold turf has just been laid o'er him, That can tell how be-loved was the soul that's fled, Or how deep in our hearts we de-plore him: 'T is the tear thro' ma-ny a

* These lines were occasioned by the loss of a very near and dear relative.

long day wept, Through a life by his loss all shad - ed; 'T is the sad re-

mem - brance, fond-ly kept, When all light - er griefs have fad - ed!

II.

Oh! thus shall we mourn; and his memory's light,
 While it shines through our hearts, will improve them;
For worth shall look fairer, and truth more bright,
 When we think how he lived but to love them!
And, as buried saints the grave perfume,
 Where, fadeless, they've long been lying,
So our hearts shall borrow a sweet'ning bloom
 From the image he left there in dying!

THOUGH DARK ARE OUR SORROWS.

With spirit and feeling.

AIR—ST. PATRICK'S DAY.

Tho' dark are our sor-rows, to-day we'll for-get them, And smile thro' our tears, like a sun-beam in show'rs; There nev-er were hearts, if our rul-ers would let them, More form'd to be tran-quil and blest than ours! But, just when the chain Has ceased to pain, And hope has en-wreath'd it round with flow'rs, There comes a new link Our spi-rit to sink! — Oh! the

joy that we taste, like the light of the poles, Is a flash a - mid dark - ness, too bril-liant to

stay; But tho' 't were the last lit - tle spark in our souls, We must light it up now, on our

Prin-ce's Day.

II.

Contempt on the minion who calls you disloyal!
   Though fierce to your foe, to your friends you are true;
And the tribute most high to a head that is royal,
   Is love from a heart that loves liberty too.
      While cowards, who blight
      Your fame, your right,
Would shrink from the blaze of the battle array,
      The standard of Green
      In front would be seen —
Oh! my life on your faith! were you summon'd this minute,
   You'd cast every bitter remembrance away,
And show what the arm of old Erin has in it,
   When roused by the foe, on her Prince's Day.

III.

He loves the Green Isle, and his love is recorded
   In hearts which have suffer'd too much to forget:
And hope shall be crown'd and attachment rewarded,
   And Erin's gay jubilee shine out yet.
      The gem may be broke
      By many a stroke,
But nothing can cloud its native ray,
      Each fragment will cast
      A light to the last. —
And thus Erin, my country, though broken thou art,
   There's a lustre within thee that ne'er will decay;
A spirit which beams through each suffering part,
   And now smiles at all pain on the Prince's Day.

WEEP ON, WEEP ON.

Mournfully.

AIR—THE SONG OF SORROW.

Weep on, weep on, your hour is past; Your dreams of pride are o'er; The fa- tal chain is round you cast, And you are men no more! In vain the He- ro's heart hath bled; The Sage-'s tongue hath warn'd in vain;— Oh, Freedom! once thy flame hath fled, It ne- ver lights a- gain!

II. "'Twas fate," they'll say, "a wayward fate, Y ur web of discord wove; And, while your tyrants join'd in hate, You never join'd in love. But hearts fell off that ought to twine, And man profaned what God hath given, Till some were heard to curse the shrine Where others knelt to Heaven "

SHE IS FAR FROM THE LAND.

With melancholy expression.

AIR—OPEN THE DOOR.

She is far from the land, where her young he-ro sleeps, And lov-ers are round her sigh- -ing; But cold-ly she turns from their gaze, and weeps, For her heart in his grave is ly - ing!

II.

She sings the wild songs of her dear native plains,
Every note which he loved awaking; —
Ah! little they think, who delight in her strains,
How the heart of the Minstrel is breaking.

III.

He had lived for his love, for his country he died,
They were all that to life had entwined him;
Nor soon shall the tears of his country be dried,
Nor long will his love stay behind him.

IV.

Oh! make her a grave where the sunbeams rest
When they promise a glorious morrow;
They'll shine o'er her sleep, like a smile from the West,
From her own lovèd island of sorrow.

MY NORA CREINA.

LESBIA HAS A BEAMING EYE.

AIR—NORA CREINA.

Les - bia has a beam-ing eye, But no one knows for whom it beam-eth; Right and left its ar-rows fly, But what they aim at no one dreameth! Sweeter 'tis to gaze up-on My No - ra's lid, that sel-dom ris - es; Few her looks, but

ev'-ry one, Like un-ex-pect-ed light sur-pri-es! Oh, my No-ra Crei-na dear! My

gen-tle, bash-ful No-ra Crei-na! Beau-ty lies In ma-ny eyes, But love in yours, my

No-ra Crei-na!

espress.

II.

Lesbia wears a robe of gold,
    But all so close the nymph has laced it,
Not a charm of beauty's mould
    Presumes to stay where nature placed it!
Oh! my Nora's gown for me,
    That floats as wild as mountain breezes,
Leaving ev'ry beauty free
    To sink or swell as heaven pleases!
Yes, my Nora Creina dear!
    My simple, graceful Nora Creina!
      Nature's dress
      Is loveliness,
The dress *you* wear, my Nora Creina!

III.

Lesbia has a wit refined,
    But, when its points are gleaming round us,
Who can tell if they 're design'd
    To dazzle merley, or to wound us.
Pillow'd on my Nora's heart,
    In safer slumber love reposes; —
Bed of peace! whose roughest part
    Is but the crumpling of the roses!
Oh, my Nora Creina dear!
    My mild, my artless Nora Creina!
      Wit, tho' bright,
      Has not the light
That warms your eyes, my Nora Creina!

I SAW THY FORM.

Tenderly.

AIR—DOMHNALL.

I saw thy form in youthful prime, Nor thought that pale de-cay — — Would steal be-fore the steps of time, And waste its bloom a-way, MARY! Yet still thy fea-tures wore that light Which fleets not with the breath; And life ne'er look'd more pure-ly bright Than in thy smile of death, MA-RY!

II. As streams, that run o'er golden mines, With modest murmur glide, Nor seem to know the wealth that shines Within their gentle tide, MARY! So, veil'd beneath a simple guise, Thy radiant genius shone, And that, which charm'd all other eyes, Seem'd worthless in thy own, MARY!

III. If souls could always dwell above, Thou ne'er hadst left that sphere; Or, could we keep the souls we love, We ne'er had lost thee here, MARY! Though many a gifted mind we meet, Though fairest forms we see, To live with them is far less sweet Than to remember thee, MARY!

WHAT THE BEE IS TO THE FLOWRET.

AIR—THE YELLOW HORSE.

What the bee is to the flowret, When he looks for ho - ney dew Thro' the leaves that close embower it,

That, my love, I'll be to you! What the bank, with ver - dure glow-ing, Is to waves that

wan-der near, Whisp'ring kiss-es, while they're go - ing, That I'll be to you, my dear!

7

WHAT THE BEE IS TO THE FLOWRET.

DUETTO.

What the bank, with ver - dure glow-ing, Is to waves that wan-der near, Whisp'ring kiss-es,

What the bank, with ver - dure glow-ing, Is to waves that wan-der near, Whisp'ring kiss-es,

while they're go - ing, That I'll be to you my dear!

while they're go - ing, That I'll be to you my dear!

SHE.

But, they say, the bee's a ro-ver, That he'll fly, when sweets are gone; And when once the kiss is o-ver

HE.

Faithless brooks will wan-der on! Nay, if flowers *will* lose their looks, If sun-ny banks *will*

wear a - way,   'T is but right, that bees and brooks Should sip and kiss them, while they may.

DUETTO.

Nay,   if flowers *will* lose their looks, If sun - ny banks *will* wear a - way, 'T is but right, that

Nay,   if flowers *will* lose their looks, If sun - ny banks *will* wear a - way, 'T is but right, that

bees   and brooks Should sip and kiss them, while they may.

bees   and brooks Should sip and kiss them, while they may.

BY THAT LAKE, WHOSE GLOOMY SHORE.*

AIR—THE BROWN IRISH GIRL.

By that Lake, whose gloomy shore Sky-lark nev - er warbles o'er,† Where the cliff hangs high and steep, Young Saint Ke - vin stole to sleep. "Here, at least," he calm-ly said, "Wo-man ne'er shall find my bed." Ah! the good Saint lit - tle knew What that

* This ballad is founded upon one of the many stories related of St. KEVIN, whose bed in the rock is to be seen at Glendalough, a most gloomy and romantic spot in the county of Wicklow.
† There are many other curious traditions concerning this lake, which may be found in GIRALDUS, COIGAN, &c.

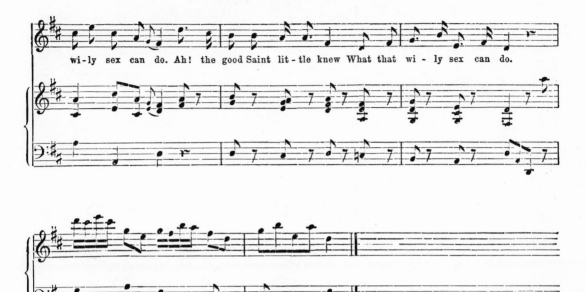

wi-ly sex can do. Ah! the good Saint lit-tle knew What that wi-ly sex can do.

II.

'Twas from Kathleen's eyes he flew, —
Eyes of most unholy blue!
She had loved him well and long,
Wish'd him hers, nor thought it wrong.
Wheresoe'er the Saint would fly,
Still he heard her light foot nigh;
East or west, where'er he turn'd,
Still her eyes before him burn'd.

III.

On the bold cliff's bosom cast,
Tranquil now he sleeps at last;
Dreams of heaven, nor thinks that e'er
Woman's smile can haunt him there.
But nor earth nor heaven is free
From her power if fond she be:
Even now, while calm he sleeps,
Kathleen o'er him leans and weeps.

IV

Fearless she had track'd his feet
To this rocky, wild retreat;
And, when morning met his view,
Her mild glances met it too.
Ah! your Saints have cruel hearts!
Sternly from his bed he starts.
And, with rude, repulsive shock,
Hurls her from the beetling rock.

V.

Glendalough! thy gloomy wave
Soon was gentle Kathleen's grave!
Soon the Saint (yet ah! too late)
Felt her love, and mourn'd her fate.
When he said, "Heaven rest her soul,"
Round the lake light music stole;
And her ghost was seen to glide,
Smiling, o'er the fatal tide!

NAY, TELL ME NOT.

AIR—DENNIS, DON'T BE THREATENING.

Nay, tell me not, dear! that the gob - let drowns One charm of feel - ing, one fond re - gret; Be-

lieve me, a few of thy an - gry frowns Are all I've sunk in its bright wave yet.

Ne'er hath a beam Been lost in the stream That e - ver was shed from thy form or soul; The

balm of thy sighs, The spell of thine eyes, Still float on the sur-face, and hal-low my bowl! Then

fan - cy not, dear-est! that wine can steal One bliss - ful dream of the heart from me; Like

founts, that a - wak - en the pil-grim's zeal, The bowl but brightens my love for thee!

II.

They tell us that Love, in his fairy bower,
  Had two blush-roses, of birth divine;
He sprinkled the one with a rainbow's shower,
  But bathed the other with mantling wine.
    Soon did the buds
    That drank of the floods
Distill'd by the rainbow decline and fade;
    While those which the tide
    Of ruby had dyed
All blush'd into beauty, like thee, sweet maid!
Then fancy not, dearest, that wine can steal
  One blissful dream of the heart from me;
Like founts that awaken the pilgrim's zeal,
  The bowl but brightens my love for thee.

AVENGING AND BRIGHT.

AIR—CROOGHAN A VENEE.*

Boldly.

A-veng-ing and bright fall the swift sword of E-rin, On him, who the

brave sons of Us-na be-tray'd! For ev'-ry fond eye which he wak-en'd a tear in, A

espress.

* The name of this beautiful and truly Irish air is, I am told, properly written *Cruachàn na Fèine,* i. e., the Fenian Mount, or mount of the Finnian heroes, those brave followers of *Finn Mac Cool,* so celebrated in the early history of our country.

The words of this song were suggested by the very ancient Irish story called "Deirdri, or the lamentable fate of the sons of Usnach," which has been translated literally from the Gaelic, by Mr. O'FLANAGAN (see Vol. 1. of Transactions of the Gaelic Society of Dublin), and upon which it appears that the "Darthula" of Macpherson is founded. The treachery of Conor, king of Ulster, in putting to death the three sons of Usna, was the cause of a desolating war against Ulster, which terminated in the destruction of Eman. "This story (says Mr. O'FLANAGAN) has been from time immemorial held in high repute as one of the three tragic stories of the Irish. These are, 'The death of the Children of Touran,' 'The death of the Children of Lear' (both regarding Tuatha de Danans), and this, 'The death of the Children of Usnach,' which is a Milesian story." — It will be recollected, that, at page 46 of these Melodies, there is a Ballad upon the story of the Children of Lear or Lir: "Silent, O Moyle!" &c.

Whatever may be thought of those sanguine claims to antiquity, which Mr. O'FLANAGAN and others advance for the literature of Ireland, it would be a very lasting reproch upon our nationality, if the Gaelic researches of this gentleman did not meet with all the liberal encouragement which they merit.

drop from his heart-wounds shall weep o'er   her   blade.

II.

By the red cloud that hung over Conor's dark dwelling,⁎

　When Ulad's⁎⁎ three champions lay sleeping in gore —

By the billows of war, which so often, high swelling,

　Have wafted these heroes to victory's shore —

III.

We swear to revenge them! — no joy shall be tasted,

　The harp shall be silent, the maiden unwed,

Our halls shall be mute and our fields shall lie wasted,

　Till vengeance is wreak'd on the murderer's head!

IV.

Yes, monarch! though sweet are our home recollections,

　Though sweet are the tears that from tenderness fall;

Though sweet are our friendships, our hopes, our affections,

　Revenge on a tyrant is sweetest of all!

⁎ "O Naisi! view the cloud that I here see in the sky! I see over Eman green a chilling cloud of blood-
tinged red." — Deirdri's Song.

⁎⁎ Ulster.

LOVE AND THE NOVICE.

HERE WE DWELL IN HOLIEST BOWERS.

Smoothly and in moderate time.

AIR—CEAN DUBH DELISH.*

"Here we dwell in ho-li-est bow-ers, Where An-gels of light o'er our o-ri-sons bend; Where sighs of de-vo-tion and breath-ing of flow-ers To hea-ven in ming-led o-dours as-cend! Do not dis-turb our calm, oh Love! So

* We have taken the liberty of omitting a part of this Air, which appeared to us to wander rather un-manageably out of the compass of the voice.

like is thy form to the che - rubs a - bove, It well might de - ceive such hearts as ours."

II.

Love stood near the Novice and listen'd,
And Love is no novice in taking a hint;
His laughing blue eyes soon with piety glisten'd;
His rosy wing turn'd to heaven's own tint.
"Who would have thought," the urchin cries,
"That Love could so well, so gravely disguise
His wandering wings and wounding eyes?"

III.

Love now warms thee, waking and sleeping,
Young Novice, to him all thy orisons rise,
He tinges the heavenly fount with his weeping,
He brightens the censer's flame with his sighs.
Love is the saint enshrined in thy breast,
And angels themselves would admit such a guest,
If he came to them clothed in Piety's vest.

THIS LIFE IS ALL CHEQUERED.

With feeling and gaiety.

AIR—THE BUNCH OF GREEN RUSHES THAT GREW AT THE BRIM.

This life is all chequ-er'd with plea-sures and woes, That chase one an - o - ther like waves of the deep, Each bil - low, as bright-ly or dark - ly it flows, Re-

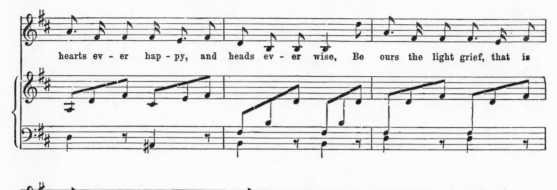

hearts ev - er hap - py, and heads ev - er wise, Be ours the light grief, that is

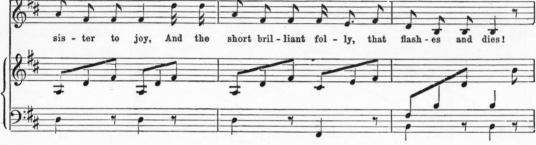

sis - ter to joy, And the short bril - liant fol - ly, that flash - es and dies!

11.

When Hylas was sent with his urn to the fount,
　　Through fields full of light, with heart full of play,
Light rambled the boy, over meadow and mount,
　　And neglected his task for the flowers on the way.*
Thus many, like me, who in youth should have tasted
　　The fountain that runs by Philosophy's shrine,
Their time with the flowers on the margin have wasted
　　And left their light urns all as empty as mine.
But pledge me the goblet — while idleness weaves
　　These flowerets together, should Wisdom but see
One bright drop or two that has fallen on the leaves
　　From her fountain divine, 't is sufficient for me.

* Proposito florem prætulit officio. — Propert. lib. i. eleg. 20.

COME, REST IN THIS BOSOM.

With melancholy feeling, but not too slow.

AIR—LOUGH SHEELING.

Come, rest in this bo-som, my own stricken deer! Tho' the herd have fled from thee, thy home is still here; Here still is the smile that no cloud can o'er-cast, And the heart and the hand all thy own to the last!

II.

Oh! what was love made for, if 't is not the same
Through joy and through torment, through glory and shame?
I know not, I ask not, if guilt's in that heart,
I but know that I love thee, whatever thou art.

III.

Thou has call'd me thy Angel in moments of bliss,
And thy Angel I'll be, 'mid the horrors of this,
Through the furnace, unshrinking, thy steps to pursue,
And shield thee, and save thee, or perish there too.

THE YOUNG MAY MOON.

AIR—THE DANDY O!

The young May moon is beam-ing, love, The glow-worm's lamp is gleam-ing, love, How sweet to rove Thro' Mor-na's grove*, While the drowsy world is dreaming, love! Then a-wake! the heav'ns look bright, my dear! 'T is nev-er too late for de-

* "Steals silently to Morna's grove." See a translation from the Irish, in Mr. Bunting's collection, by John Brown, one of my earliest college companions and friends, whose death was as singularly melancholy and unfortunate as his life has been amiable, honourable, and exemplary.

light, my dear! And the best of all ways To leng-then our days, Is to steal a few hours from the

night, my dear!

II.

Now all the world is sleeping, love,
But the Sage, his star-watch keeping, love,
    And I whose star,
    More glorious far,
Is the eye from that casement peeping, love.
Then awake! — till rise of sun, my dear,
The Sage's glass we'll shun, my dear,
    Or, in watching the flight
    Of bodies of light,
He might happen to take thee for one, my dear.

OH THE SHAMROCK!

AIR—ALLEY CROKER.

In moderate time.

E-RIN's Isle, To sport a-while, As LOVE and VAL-OUR wan - der'd, With WIT, the sprite, Whose

quiv-er bright A thou-sand ar - rows sqan - der'd; Where'er they pass, A trip - le grass* Shoots

up, with dewdrops streaming, As soft-ly green As em'-ralds seen, Thro' purest crystal gleam - ing!

* SAINT PATRICK is said to have made use of that species of the trefoil, to which in Ireland we give the name of Shamrock, in explaining the doctrine of the Trinity to the pagan Irish. I do not know if there be any other reason for our adoption of this plant as a national emblem. HOPE, among the ancients, was sometimes represented as a beautiful child, "standing upon tip-toes, and a trefoil or three-coloured grass in her hand."

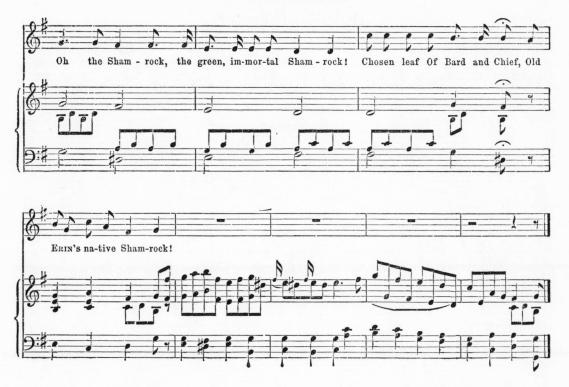

Oh the Sham-rock, the green, im-mor-tal Sham-rock! Chosen leaf Of Bard and Chief, Old

Erin's na-tive Sham-rock!

II.

Says Valour, "See,
They spring for me,
Those leafy gems of morning!" —
Says Love, "No, no,
For me they grow,
My fragrant path adorning,"
But Wit perceives
The triple leaves,
And cries, "Oh! do not sever
A type that blends
Three godlike friends,
Love, Valour, Wit, for ever!"
the Shamrock, the green, immortal Shamrock!
Chosen leaf
Of Bard and Chief,
Old Erin's native Shamrock!

III.

So firmly fond
May last the bond
They wove that morn together,
And ne'er may fall
One drop of gall
On Wit's celestial feather!
May Love, as twine
His flowers divine,
Of thorny falsehood weed 'em!
May Valour ne'er
His standard rear
Against the cause of Freedom!
O the Shamrock, the green, immortal Shamrock!
Chosen leaf
Of Bard and Chief,
Old Erin's native Shamrock!

THE MINSTREL BOY.

With strength and spirit.

AIR—THE MOREEN.

Min - strel Boy to the war is gone, In the ranks of death you 'll find him; His

fa - ther's sword he has gird - ed on, And his wild harp slung be - hind him.

II.

The Minstrel fell! — but the foeman's chain
Could not bring that proud soul under;
The harp he loved ne'er spoke again,
For he tore its chords asunder;
And said, "No chains shall sully thee,
"Thou soul of love and bravery!
"Thy songs were made for the pure and free,
"They shall never sound in slavery."

I'D MOURN THE HOPES THAT LEAVE ME.

Tenderly.

AIR—THE ROSE TREE.

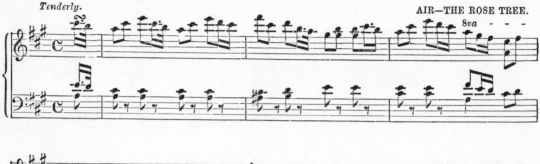

I'd mourn the hopes that leave me, If *thy* smiles had

left me too; I'd weep, when friends de-ceive me, If *thou* wert, like them, un-true.

ad lib.

But, while I've thee be-fore me, With heart so warm and eye so bright, No

a tempo.

clouds can linger o'er me That smile turns them all to light!

II.

'Tis not in fate to harm me,
  While fate leaves thy love to me;
'Tis not in joy to charm me,
  Unless joy be shared with thee.
One minute's dream about thee,
  Were worth a long and endless year
Of waking bliss without thee,
  My own love, my only dear!

III.

And though the hope be gone, love,
  That long sparkled o'er our way,
Oh! we shall journey on, love,
  More safely without its ray.
Far better lights shall win me
  Along the path I've yet to roam —
The mind that burns within me,
And pure smiles from thee at home

IV.

Thus, when the lamp that lighted
  The traveller at first goes out,
He feels awhile benighted,
  And looks around in fear and doubt.
But soon, the prospect clearing,
  By cloudless starlight on he treads,
And thinks no lamp so cheering
  As that light which Heaven sheds.

THE TIME I'VE LOST IN WOOING.

Lightly and in moderate time.

AIR—PEASE UPON A TRENCHER.

The time I've lost in woo-ing, In watch-ing and pur-su-ing The light that lies In Wo-man's eyes, Has been my heart's un-do-ing. Tho'

Wis-dom oft has sought me, I scorn'd the lore she brought me; My on-ly books Were

Woman's looks, And Fol - ly's all they've taught me.

II.

Her smile when Beauty granted,
I hung with gaze enchanted,
   Like him the Sprite*
   Whom maids by night
Oft meet in glen that's haunted.
Like him, too, Beauty won me,
But while her eyes were on me,
   If once their ray
   Was turn'd away,
Oh! winds could not outrun me.

III.

And are those follies going?
And is my proud heart growing
   Too cold or wise
   For brilliant eyes
Again to set it glowing?
No—vain, alas! th' endeavour
From bonds so sweet to sever; —
   Poor Wisdom's chance
   Against a glance
Is now as weak as ever.

---

* This alludes to a kind of Irish Fairy, which is to be met with, they say, in the fields, at dusk; — as long as you keep your eyes upon him, he is fixed and in your power; but the moment you look away (and he is ingenious in furnishing some inducement), he vanishes. I had thought that this was the sprite which we call the Leprechaun; but a high authority upon such subjects, Lady MORGAN (in a note upon her national and interesting novel, O'Donnel), has given a very different account of that Goblin.

NO, NOT MORE WELCOME.

AIR—LUGGELAW.

No, not more wel - come the fai-ry num - bers Of mu-sic fall on the sleep-er's ear, When half a-wak - ing from fear - ful slum - bers, He thinks the full quire of heav'n is

near, — Then came that voice, when, all for-sak-en, This heart long had sleep-ing

lain, Nor thougth its cold pulse would ev-er wak-en To such be'-nign, bless-ed sounds a-

gain.

II.

Sweet voice of comfort! 'twas like the stealing
  Of summer wind through some wreathèd shell —
Each secret winding, each inmost feeling
  Of all my soul echoed to its spell! —
'T was whisper'd balm — 'twas sunshine spoken. —
  I'd live years of grief and pain
To have my long sleep of sorrow broken
  By such benign, blessed sounds again.

DEAR HARP OF MY COUNTRY.

Moderate time, and with much warmth of expression.

AIR—NEW LANGOLEE.

Dear Harp of my Country! in dark-ness I found thee, The cold chain of si-lence* had

hung o'er thee long, When proud-ly, my own Is-land Harp! I un-bound thee, And

gave all thy chords to light, free-dom and song! The warm lay of love and the

* In that rebellious but beautiful song—"When Erin first rose," there is, if I recollect right, the following line:—
"The dark chain of silence was thrown o'er the deep."

The Chain of Silence was a sort of practical figure of rhetoric among the ancient Irish. Walker tells us of "a celebrated contention for precedence between Finn and Gaul, near Finn's palace at Almhaim, where the attending Bards, anxious, if possible, to produce a cessation of hostilities, shook the Chain of Silence, and flung themselves among the ranks." See also the Ode to Gaul, the son of Morni, in Miss Brook's *Reliques of Irish Poetry.*

light note of glad-ness Have wak-en'd thy [fond-est, thy live-li-est thrill; But so

lentando.   *espress.*

oft hast thou e-cho'd the deep sigh of sad-ness, That ev'n in thy mirth it will

steal from thee still.

II.

Dear Harp of my Country! farewell to thy numbers,
　This sweet wreath of song is the last we shall twine;
Go, — sleep, with the sunshine of Fame on thy slumbers,
　Till touch'd by some hand less unworthy than mine.
If the pulse of the patriot, soldier, or lover,
　Have throbb'd at our lay, 't is thy glory alone;
I was but as the wind, passing heedlessly over,
　And all the wild sweetness I waked was thy own!

AT THE MID HOUR OF NIGHT.

Slow, and with melancholy expression.

AIR—MOLLY, MY DEAR.

At the mid hour of night, when stars are weep-ing, I fly To the lone vale we loved, when

life shone warm in thine eye; And I think that, if spir-its can steal from the

re-gion of air To re-vi-sit past scenes of de-light, thou wilt come to me there, And

tell me our love is re-mem-ber'd ev'n in the sky!

2ND VERSE.

Then i sing the wild song, which once 'twas rap-ture to hear, When our voi-ces, both

mingl-ing, breath'd like one on the ear; And, as E-cho far off through the vale my sad

o - ri - son, rolls, I think, oh my love! 'tis thy voice from the king-dom of souls,* Faintly

an - swer-ing still the notes that once were so dear!

* "There are countries," says MONTAIGNE, "where they believe the souls of the happy live in all manner of liberty, in delightful fields; and that it is those souls repeating the words we utter, which we call Echo."

ONE BUMPER AT PARTING.

With animation.

AIR—MOLL ROE IN THE MORNING.

One bum-per at parting!—tho' ma-ny Have cir-cled the board since we met, The full-est, the sad-dest of a-ny Re-mains to be crown'd by as yet. The sweet-ness that plea-sure has in it, Is al-ways so slow to come forth, That sel-dom, a-las, till the mi-nute It

dies, do we know half its worth! But, oh! may our life's hap-py mea-sure Be

all of such moments made up; They're born on the bo-som of Plea-sure. They

die midst the tears of the cup.

As onward we journey, how pleasant
   To pause and inhabit awhile
Those few sunny spots, like the present,
   That 'mid the dull wilderness smile!
But time, like a pitiless master,
   Cries "Onward!" and spurs the gay hours —
Ah, never doth time travel faster,
   Than when his way lies among flowers.
But come—may our life's happy measure
   Be all of such moments made up;
They're born on the bosom of Pleasure,
   They die 'midst the tears of the cup,

We saw how the sun look'd in sinking,
   The waters beneath him how bright,
And now let our farewell of drinking
   Resemble that farewell of light.
You saw how he finish'd, by darting,
   His beam o'er a deep billow's brim
So, fill up, let's shine at our parting,
   In full, liquid glory, like him.
And oh! may our life's happy measure
   Of moments like this be made up;
'Twas born in the bosom of Pleasure,
   It dies 'mid the tears of the cup.

9

THE VALLEY LAY SMILING BEFORE ME.

THE SONG OF O'RUARK. PRINCE OF BREFFNI.*

According to the feeling of each verse. AIR—THE PRETTY GIRL MILKING HER COW.

The val-ley lay smi-ling be-fore me, Where late-ly I left her be-hind; Yet I

trembled, and some-thing hung o'er me, That sad-den'd the joy of my mind. I

* These stanzas are founded upon an event of most melancholy importance to Ireland; if, as we are told by our Irish historians, it gave England the first opportunity of profiting by our divisions and subduing us. The following are the circumstances as related by O'Halloran: — "The King of Leinster had long conceived a violent affection for Dearbhorgil, daughter to the King of Meath, 'and though she had been for some time married to O'Ruark, Prince of Breffni, yet could it not restrain his passion. They carried on a private correspondence, and she informed him that O'Ruark intended soon to go on a pilgrimage (an act of piety frequent in those days), and conjured him to embrace that opportunity of conveying her from a husband she detested to a lover she adored. Mac Murchad too punctually obeyed the summons, and had the lady conveyed to his capital of Ferns." — The monarch Roderic espoused the cause of O'Ruark, while Mac Murchad fled to England, and obtained the assistance of Henry II.

look'd for the lamp, which she told me Should shine when her pil-grim re-

turn'd, But, tho' dark-ness be-gan to in-fold me. No lamp from the bat-tle-ments burn'd.

II.

I flew to her chamber — 'twas lonely,
 As if the loved tenant lay dead; —
Ah, would it were death, and death only!
 But no, the young false one had fled.
And there hung the lute that could soften
 My very worst pains into bliss,
While the hand that had waked it so often
 Now throbb'd to a proud rival's kiss.

III.

There *was* a time, falsest of women!
 When Breffni's good sword would have sought
That man, through a million of foemen,
 Who dared but to wrong thee *in thought!*
While now — O degenerate daughter
 Of Erin, how fallen is thy fame!
And through ages of bondage and slaughter,
 Our country shall bleed for thy shame.

IV.

Already the curse is upon her.
 And strangers her valleys profane;
They come to divide — to dishonour,
 And tyrants they long will remain.
But onward! — the green banner rearing,
 Go, flesh every sword to the hilt;
On *our* side is Virtue and Erin,
 On *theirs* is the Saxon and guilt.

OH! HAD WE SOME BRIGHT LITTLE ISLE.

With lightness, and in moderate time.

AIR—SHEELA NA GUIRA.

Oh! had we some bright lit-tle Isle of our own In a blue sum-mer o-cean, far off and a-lone; Where a leaf ne-ver dies in the still-blooming bow'rs, And the bee ban-quets on thro' a whole year of

flow'rs. Where the sun loves to pause With so fond a de - lay, That the
night on - ly draws A thin veil o'er the day; Where sim - ply to feel that we
breathe, that we live, Is worth the best joy that life else - where can give.

II.

There with souls ever ardent and pure as the clime,
We should love as they loved in the first golden time;
The glow of the sunshine, the balm of the air,
Would steal to our hearts, and make all summer there.
With affection as free
From decline as the bowers,
And with hope, like the bee,
Living always on flowers,
Our life should resemble a long day of light,
And our death come on holy and calm as the night.

FAREWELL! BUT, WHENEVER YOU WELCOME THE HOUR.

With expression.

AIR—MOLL ROONE.

Farewell!—but, when-e-ver you wel-come the hour, Which a-wak-ens the nigth-song of mirth in your bower, Then think of the friend, who once wel-comed it too, And for-got his own griefs to be hap-py with you.

His griefs may re-turn—not a hope may re-main Of the few that have brighten'd his

path-way of pain—But he ne'er will for-get the short vi-sion, that threw its en-

chantment a-round him, while ling'-ring with you!

II.

And still on that evening, when pleasure fills up
To the highest top sparkle each heart and each cup,
Where'er my path lies, be it gloomy or bright,
My soul, happy friends, shall be with you that night;
Shall join in your revels, your sports, and your wiles,
And return to me beaming all o'er with your smiles —
Too blest, if it tells me, that 'mid the gay cheer,
Some kind voice had murmur'd, "I wish he were here!"

III.

Let Fate do her worst; there are relics of joy,
Bright dreams of the past, which she cannot destroy,
Which come in the night-time of sorrow and care,
And bring back the features that joy used to wear.
Long, long be my heart with such memories fill'd!
Like the vase, in which roses have once been distill'd —
You may break, you may shatter the vase if you will,
But the scent of the roses will hang round it still.

OH! DOUBT ME NOT.

With feeling and cheerfulness.

AIR—YELLOW WAT AND THE FOX.

Oh! doubt me not, the sea-son Is o'er, when Fol-ly made me rove, And

now the ves-tal Rea-son Shall watch the fire a-wak'd by Love, Al-tho' this heart was

ear-ly blown, And fair-est hands dis-turb'd the tree, They on-ly shook some blossoms down, Its

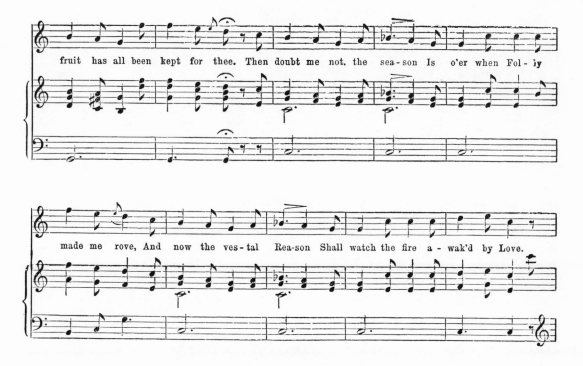

fruit has all been kept for thee. Then doubt me not, the sea-son Is o'er when Fol-ly

made me rove, And now the ves-tal Rea-son Shall watch the fire a-wak'd by Love.

II.

And though my lute no longer

    May sing of Passion's ardent spell,

Yet, trust me, all the stronger

    I feel the bliss I do not tell.

The bee through many a garden roves,

    And hums his lay of courtship o'er,

But, when he finds the flower he loves,

    He settles there, and hums no more.

Then doubt me not—the season

    Is o'er when Folly kept me free,

And now the vestal, Reason,

    Shall guard the flame awaked by thee.

COME O'ER THE SEA.

With impassioned melancholy.

AIR—CUSHLA MA CHREE.*

Come o'er the sea, Maid-en! with me, Mine thro' sun-shine, storm, and snows! Sea-sons may roll, But the true soul Burns the same, wher-e'er it goes. Let For-tune frown, so we love and part not; 'T is life where *thou* art, 't is

* The following are some of the original words of this wild and singular Air; — they contain rather an odd assortment of grievances.

Cushla ma chree,
Did you but see
How, the rogue, he did serve me; — *Bis.*
He broke my pitcher, he spilt my water,
He kiss'd my wife, and he married my daughter!
O Cushla ma chree! &c.

death where thou art not! Then come o'er the Sea, Maiden! with me, Come wher-ev-er the

wild wind blows; Sea-sons may roll, But the true soul Burns the same, wher-

e'er it goes.

II.

Was not the sea
Made for the Free,
Land for courts and chains alone?
Here we are slaves,
But, on the waves,
Love and liberty's all our own.
No eye to watch, and no tongue to wound us,
All earth forgot, and all heaven around us —
Then come o'er the sea,
Maiden, with me,
Mine through sunshine, storm, and snows;
Seasons may roll,
But the true soul
Burns the same, where'er it goes.

OH! COULD WE DO WITH THIS WORLD OF OURS.

Lively.

AIR—BASKET OF OYSTERS.

Oh! could we do with this world of ours As thou dost with thy gar - den bow'rs, Re-

ject the weeds and keep the flow'rs, What a hea - ven on earth we'd make it! So

bright a dwell - ing should be our own, So war - rant - ed free from

sigh or frown, That an-gels soon would be com-ing down, By the

week or month to take it.

II.

Like those gay flies that wing thro' air,
And in themselves a lustre bear,
A stock of light, still ready there,
    Whenever they wish to use it; —
So, in this world I'd make for thee,
Our hearts should all like fire-flies be,
And the flash of wit or poesy
    Break forth whenever we choose it.

III.

While ev'ry joy that glads our sphere
Hath still some shadow hov'ring near,
In this new world of ours, my dear,
    Such shadows will all be omitted: —
Unless they 're like that graceful one
Which, when thou 'rt dancing in the sun,
Still near thee, leaves a charm upon
    Each spot where it hath flitted.

HAS SORROW THY YOUNG DAYS SHADED.

Simply and tenderly.

AIR—SLY PATRICK.

Has sor-row thy young days shad-ed, As clouds o'er the morn-ing fleet? — Too fast have those young days fad-ed, That e-ven in sor-row were sweet. — Does Time, with his cold wing wi - ther Each

feel - ing that once was dear? — Then, child of mis - for - tune, come hi - ther, I'll weep with thee,

tear for tear.

II.

Has love to that soul, so tender,
  Been like a Lagenian mine,*
Where sparkles of golden splendour
  All over the surface shine?
But, if in pursuit we go deeper,
  Allured by the gleam that shone,
Ah! false as the dream of the sleeper,
  Like Love, the bright ore is gone.

III.

Has Hope, like the bird in the story,†
  That flitted from tree to tree
With the talisman's glittering glory —
  Has Hope been that bird to thee?
On branch after branch alighting,
  The gem did she still display,
And, when nearest and most inviting,
  Then waft the fair gem away?

IV

If thus the young hours have fleeted,
  When sorrow itself look'd bright;
If thus the fair hope hath cheated,
  That led thee along so light;
If thus the cold world now wither
  Each feeling that once was dear: —
Come, child of misfortune, come hither,
  I'll weep with thee, tear for tear.

* Our Wicklow gold-mines, to which this verse alludes, deserve, I fear, the character here given of them.
† "The bird, having got its prize, settled not far off, with the talisman in his mouth. The prince drew near it, hoping it would drop it; but, as he approached, the bird took wing, and settled again," &c. — Arabian Nights, Story of Kummir al Zummaun and the Princess of China.

LAY HIS SWORD BY HIS SIDE.

With melancholy feeling and energy.

AIR—IF THE SEA WERE INK.

Lay his sword by his side —* it hath served him too well, Not to rest near his pil - low be - low; To the last mo - ment true, from his hand ere it fell, Its point still was turn'd to a fly - ing foe. Fel - low - lab'-rers in life, let them

* It was the custom of the ancient Irish, in the manner of the Scythians, to bury the favourite swords of their heroes along with them.

slumber in death, Side by side, as be-comes the re-pos-ing brave, — The sword which he

loved still un - broke in its sheath, And him-self un-sub-dued in his grave.

II.

Yet pause — for, in fancy, a still voice I hear,
　As if breath'd from his brave heart's remains; —
Faint echo of that which in Slavery's ear
　Once sounded the war-word, "Burst your chains!"
And it cries, from the grave where the Hero lies deep,
　"Tho' the day of your Chieftain for ever hath set,
Oh leave not his sword thus in-glorious to sleep, —
　It hath Victory's life in it yet.

III.

"Should some alien, unworthy such weapon to wield,
　Dare to touch thee, my own gallant sword,
Then rest in thy sheath, like a talisman seal'd,
　Or return to the grave of thy chainless lord.
But, if grasp'd by a hand that hath known the bright use
　Of a falchion, like thee, on the battle plain,
Then, at Liberty's summons, like lightning let loose,
　Leap forth from thy dark sheath again!"

10

WHEN FIRST I MET THEE.

In moderate time.

AIR—O PATRICK, FLY FROM ME.*

When first I met thee, warm and young, There shone such truth a - bout thee, And on thy lip such pro - mise hung, I did not dare to doubt thee. I saw thee change, yet still re - lied, Still clung with hope the fond - er, And thought, tho' false to all be - side, From me thou couldst not

* This very beautiful Irish air was sent to me by a gentleman of Oxford. There is much pathos in the original words, and both words and music have all the features of authenticity.

wan - der. But go, de - ceiv - er! go,— The heart whose hopes could make it

Trust one so false, so low, De - serves that thou shouldst break it!

II.

When every tongue thy follies named,
  I fled th' unwelcome story;
Or found, in ev'n the faults they blamed,
  Some gleams of future glory.
I still was true, when nearer friends
  Conspired to wrong, to slight thee;
The heart, that now thy falsehood rends,
  Would then have bled to right thee.
    But go, deceiver! go,—
    Some day, perhaps, thou 'lt waken
  From pleasure's dream, to know
    The grief of hearts forsaken.

III.

Ev'n now, though youth its bloom has shed,
  No lights of age adorn thee;
The few, who loved thee once, have fled,
  And they who flatter scorn thee.
Thy midnight cup is pledged to slaves,
  No genial ties enwreath it;
The smiling there, like light on graves,
  Has rank, cold hearts beneath it!
    Go—go—though worlds were thine,
    I would not now surrender
  One taintless tear of mine
    For all thy guilty splendour!

IV.

And days may come, thou false one! yet,
  When ev'n those ties shall sever;
When thou wilt call, with vain regret,
  On her thou 'st lost for ever!
On her who, in thy fortune's fall,
  With smiles had still received thee,
And gladly died to prove thee all
  Her fancy first believed thee.
    Go—go—'t is vain to curse,
    'T is weakness to upbraid thee;
  Hate cannot wish thee worse
    Than guilt and shame have made thee.

WHILE HISTORY'S MUSE.

Moderate time with energy.

AIR—PADDY WHACK.

While His-to-ry's Muse the me - mo - rial was keeping Of

all that the dark hand of Des - ti - ny weaves, Be-side her the Ge-nius of E - rin stood weeping, For

hers was the sto-ry that blot-ted the leaves. But, oh! how the tear in her eye-lids grew bright, When,

af-ter whole pag-es of sor-row and shame, She saw His-to-ry write, With a pen-cil of

light, That il-lumed all the vol-ume, her WELLINGTON'S name!

II.

"Hail, Star of my Isle!" said the Spirit, all sparkling
  With beams such as break from her own dewy skies—
"Through ages of sorrow, deserted and darkling,
  I've watch'd for some glory like thine to arise.
For though Heroes I've number'd, unblest was their lot,
  And unhallow'd they sleep in the cross-ways of Fame;—
      But oh! there is not
      One dishonouring blot
On the wreath that encircles my Wellington's name?

III.

"Yet still the last crown of thy toils is remaining,
  The grandest, the purest, even *thou* hast yet known;
Though proud was thy task, other nations unchaining,
  Far prouder to heal the deep wounds of thy own.
At the foot of that throne for whose weal thou hast stood,
  Go, plead for the land that first cradled thy fame—
      And, bright o'er the flood
      Of her tears and her blood,
Let the rainbow of Hope be her Wellington's name!"

'T IS GONE, AND FOR EVER.

AIR—SAVOURNAH DEELISH.

'T is gone, and for ev - er, The light we saw breaking, Like Hea-ven's first dawn o'er the

sleep of the dead, When man, from the slum-ber of a - ges a - wak-ing, Look'd

up - ward and bless'd the pure ray ere it fled! 'T is gone, and the gleams it has

left of its burning, But deep-en the long night of bondage and mourning, That dark o'er the

kingdoms of earth is re - turn-ing, And, dark-est of all, hap-less E - rin! o'er thee.

II.

For high was thy hope, when those glories were darting
　Around thee, through all the gross clouds of the world;
When Truth, from her fetters indignantly starting,
　At once, like a sunburst, her banner unfurl'd.
Oh, never shall earth see a moment so splendid!
Then, then, had one Hymn of Deliverance blended
The tongues of all nations, how sweet had ascended
　The first note of Liberty, Erin! from thee.

III.

But shame on those tyrants, who envied the blessing!
　And shame on the light race, unworthy its good,
Who, at Death's reeking altar, like furies caressing
　The young hope of Freedom, baptized it in blood.
Then vanish'd for ever that fair, sunny vision,
Which, spite of the slavish, the cold heart's derision,
Shall long be remember'd, pure, bright, and elysian,
　As first it arose, my lost Erin! on thee.

OH! WHERE'S THE SLAVE.

Spirited.

AIR—SIOS AGUS SIOS LIOM.

Oh! where's the slave, so low - ly, Con-

demn'd to chains un - ho - ly, Who, could he burst His bonds at first, Would pine be-

neath them slow - ly? What soul, whose wrongs de - grade it, Would wait till time de-

cay'd, it, When thus its wing At once may spring To the throne of Him wh

made it?

*Fare-well, E - rin!

fare-well, all Who live to weep our fall!

II.

Less dear the laurel growing
Alive, untouch'd, and blowing,
Than that whose braid
Is pluck'd to shade
The brows with victory glowing.
We tread the land that bore us,
Her green flag glitters o'er us,
The friends we've tried
Are by our side,
And the foe we hate before us.
Farewell, Erin, — farewell, all
Who live to weep our fall.

* The few bars which I have here taken the liberty of connecting with this spirited Air, form one of those melancholy strains of our Music, which are called *Dumps*. I found it in a collection entitled "The Hibernian Muse," and we are told in the Essay prefixed to that Work, that "it is said to have been sung by the Irish Women on the field of battle, after a terrible slaughter made by Cromwell's troops in Ireland."

FILL THE BUMPER FAIR.

AIR—BOB AND JOAN.

Fill the bum - per fair! Ev - 'ry drop we sprin - kle O'er the brow of Care

Smooths a - way a wrin - kle. Wit's e - lec - tric flame Ne'er so swift - ly pass - es,

As when thro' the frame It shoots from brim - ming glass - es. Fill the bum - per fair!

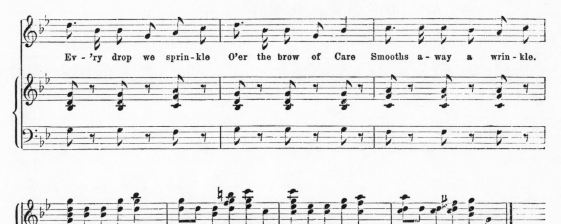

Ev - 'ry drop we sprin-kle O'er the brow of Care Smooths a - way a wrin-kle.

II.

Sages can, they say,
　Grasp the lightning's pinions,
And bring down its ray
　From the starr'd dominions: —
So we, Sages, sit
　And 'mid bumpers brightening,
From the heaven of Wit
　Draw down all its lightning.
Fill the bumper, &c.

III.

Wouldst thou know what first
　Made our souls inherit
This ennobling thirst
　For wine's celestial spirit?
It chanced upon that day,
　When, as bards inform us,
Prometheus stole away
　The living fires that warm us.
Fill the bumper, &c.

IV.

The careless Youth, when up
　To Glory's fount aspiring,
Took nor urn nor cup
　To hide the pilfer'd fire in. —
But oh, his joy! when, round
　The halls of heaven spying,
Among the stars he found
　A bowl of Bacchus lying.
Fill the bumper, &c.

V.

Some drops were in that bowl,
　Remains of last night's pleasure
With which the Sparks of Soul
　Mix'd their burning treasure.
Hence the goblet's shower
　Hath such spells to win us;
Hence its mighty power
　O'er that flame within us.
Fill the bumper, &c.

AS SLOW OUR SHIP HER FOAMY TRACK.

In moderate time and with expression.

AIR—THE GIRL I LEFT BEHIND ME.

As slow our ship her foam-y track A-gainst the wind was cleav-ing, Her trembling pen-nant still look'd back To that dear isle 't was leav-ing. So loath we part from all we love, From all the links that bind us; So

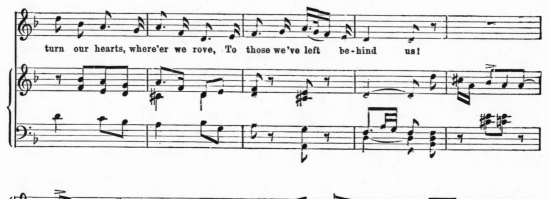

turn   our hearts, where'er we rove, To   those we've left   be - hind   us!

II.

When, round the bowl, of vanish'd years
  We talk, with joyous seeming,
And smiles that might as well be tears,
  So faint, so sad their beaming;
While memory brings us back again
  Each early tie that twined us,
Oh sweet 's the cup that circles then
  To those we 've left behind us!

III.

And, when in other climes we meet
  Some isle or vale enchanting,
Where all looks flowery, wild, and sweet,
  And nought but love is wanting;
We think how great had been our bliss,
  If Heaven had but assign'd us
To live and die in scenes like this,
  With some we 've left behind us!

IV.

As trav'llers oft look back, at eve,
  When eastward darkly going,
To gaze upon that light they leave
  Still faint behind them glowing, —
So, when the close of pleasure's day
  To gloom hath near consign'd us,
We turn to catch one fading ray
  Of joy that 's left behind us.

IN THE MORNING OF LIFE.

AIR—THE LITTLE HARVEST ROSE.

In the morn-ing of life, when its cares are un-known, And its pleasures in all their new

lus-tre be-gin; When we live in a bright-beaming world of our own, And the light that sur-

rounds us is all from with-in; Oh 't is not, be-lieve me, in that hap-py time We can

love, as in hours of less trans-port we may; Of our smiles, of our hopes, 't is the

gay sun-ny prime, But af-fec-tion is warm-est when these fade a-way.

II.

When we see the first charm of our youth pass us by,
  Like a leaf on the stream that will never return;
When our cup, which had sparkled with pleasure so high,
  Now tastes of the *other*, the dark-flowing urn;
Then, then is the moment affection can sway
  With a depth and a tenderness joy never knew;
Love, nursed among pleasures, is faithless as they,
  But the Love, born of Sorrow, like Sorrow is true!

III

In climes full of sunshine, though splendid their dyes,
  Yet faint is the odour the flowers shed about;
'T is the clouds and the mists of our own weeping skies,
  That call their full spirit of fragrancy out.
So the wild glow of passion may kindle from mirth,
  But 't is only in grief true affection appears; —
To the magic of smiles it may first owe its birth,
  But the soul of its sweetness is drawn out by tears!

WREATH THE BOWL.

AIR—NORAN KITSA.

Gaily and brilliantly.

Wreath the bowl With flow'rs of soul The bright- est Wit can find us; We'll take a flight Tow'rds Heav'n to-night, And leave dull earth be - hind us! Should Love a - mid The wreaths be hid, Which Mirth, th'enchant - er, brings us, No dan-ger fear, While wine is near, We'll drown him if he stings us. Then wreath the bowl With flow'rs of soul The

brightest Wit can find us; We'll take a flight Tow'rds heav'n to - night, And leave dull earth be-

hind us!

II.

'T was nectar fed,
Of old, 't is said,
Their Junos, Joves, Apollos;
And Man may brew
His nectar too,
The rich receipt's as follows: —
Take wine like this,
Let looks of bliss
Around it well be blended,
Then bring Wit's beam
To warm the stream,
And there's your nectar, splendid!
So wreath the bowl, &c.

III.

Say, why did Time
His glass sublime
Fill up with sands unsightly,
When wine, he knew,
Runs brisker through,
And sparkles far more brightly.
Oh, lend it us,
And, smiling thus,
The glass in two we'd sever,
Make pleasure glide
In double tide,
And fill both ends for ever!
Then wreath the bowl, &c.

11

I SAW FROM THE BEACH.

In moderate time.

AIR—MISS MOLLY.

lentando.

I saw from the beach, when the morn-ing was shin-ing, A bark o'er the wa-ters, move glo-rious-ly on; I came when the sun o'er that beach was de-clin-ing, The bark was still there, but the wa-ters were gone! I came when the sun o'er that

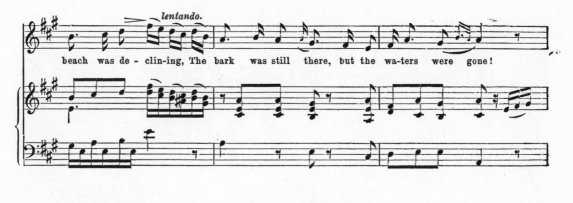

beach was de - clin-ing, The bark was still there, but the wa-ters were gone!

II.

Ah! such is the fate of our life's early promise,
    So passing the spring-tide of joy we have known;
Each wave that we danced on at morning ebbs from us,
    And leaves us, at eve, on the bleak shore alone.

III.

Ne'er tell me of glories, serenely adorning
    The close of our day, the calm eve of our night; —
Give me back, give me back the wild freshness of Morning,
    Her clouds and her tears are worth Ev'ning's best light.

IV.

Oh! who would not welcome that moment's returning,
    When passion first waked a new life through his frame,
And his soul, like the wood that grows precious in burning,
    Gave out all its sweets to love's exquisite flame!

WHEN COLD IN THE EARTH.

Slow and with melancholy expression.

AIR—LIMERICK'S LAMENTATION.*

When cold in the earth lies the friend thou hast loved, Be his faults and his fol-lies for-got by thee then; Or, if from their slum-ber the veil be re - moved, Weep o'er them in si - lence and close it a - gain. And

---

* Our right to this fine Air (the "Lochaber" of the Scotch) will, I fear, be disputed; but, as it has been long connected with Irish words, and is confidently claimed for us by Mr. Bunting and others, I thought I should not be authorized in leaving it out of this collection.

oh! if 't is pain to re - mem - ber how far From the path-ways of light he was

tempt-ed to roam, Be it bliss to re - mem-ber that thou wert the star Which a-

rose on his dark-ness, And guid-ed him home.

II.

From thee and thy innocent beauty first came
  The revealings that taught him true Love to adore,
To feel the bright presence, and turn him with shame
  From the idols he darkly had knelt to before.
O'er the waves of a life, long benighted and wild,
  Thou cam'st, like a soft golden calm o'er the sea;
And if happiness purely and glowingly smiled
  On his ev'ning horizon, the light was from thee

III.

And though sometimes the shade of past folly would rise,
  And though falsehood again would allure him to stray,
He but turn'd to the glory that dwelt in those eyes,
  And the folly, the falsehood, soon vanish'd away.
As the Priests of the Sun, when their altar grew dim,
  At the day-beam alone could its lustre repair,
So, if virtue a moment grew languid in him,
  He but flew to that smile, and rekindled it there!

TO LADIES' EYES.

In moderate time and with spirit.

AIR—FAGUE A BALLAGH.

To La-dies' eyes a-round, Boy, We can't re-fuse, we can't re-fuse, Tho' bright eyes so a-

bound, Boy, 'T is hard to choose, 't is hard to choose. For thick as stars that light-en Yon

air-y bow'rs, yon air-y bow'rs, The countless eyes that bright-en This earth of ours, this.

earth of ours. But fill the cup, wher-e'er, Boy, Our choice may fall, our choice may fall, We're

con spirito.

sure to find Love there, Boy, So drink them all! so drink them all!

II.

Some eyes there are, so holy,
　　They seem but giv'n, they seem but giv'n,
As splendid beacons, solely,
　　To light to heav'n, to light to heav'n!
While some—oh! ne'er believe them—
　　With tempting ray, with tempting ray,
Would lead us (God forgive them!)
　　The other way, the other way.
　　　　But fill the cup, &c.

III.

In some, as in a mirror,
　　Love seems portray'd, Love seems portray'd,
But shun the flattering error,
　　'T is but his shade, 't is but his shade.
Himself has fix'd his dwelling
　　In eyes we know, in eyes we know,
And lips—but this is telling,
　　So here they go! so here they go!
　　　　Fill up, fill up, &c.

FORGET NOT THE FIELD.

AIR—THE LAMENTATION OF AUGHRIM.

Despondingly.

For - get not the field where they perish'd, The tru - est, the last of the brave— All

gone! and the bright hope we cher-ish'd Gone with them, and quench'd in their grave.

2ND VERSE.

Oh! could we from death but re - cov - er Those

hearts, as   they bound-ed   be-fore,   In the face   of   high heav'n to fight o-ver   That

com - bat   for   Free-dom   once more; —

III.

Could the chain for an instant be riven
Which Tyranny flung round us then,
Oh! 't is not in Man nor in Heav'n
To let Tyranny bind it again!

IV.

But 't is past—and though blazon'd in story
The name of our Victor may be,
Accurst is the march of that glory
Which treads o'er the hearts of the free.

V.

Far dearer the grave or the prison,
Illumed by one patriot name,
Than the trophies of all who have risen
On Liberty's ruins to fame!

THEY MAY RAIL AT THIS LIFE.

With gaiety and feeling.

AIR—NOCH BONIN SHIN DOE.

They may rail at this life — from the hour I be-gan it, I've found it a life full of

kind-ness and bliss; And un-til they can show me some hap-pi-er pla-net, More

so-cial and bright, I'll con-tent me with this. As long as the world has such

e-lo-quent eyes, As be-fore me this mo-ment en-rap-tur'd I see, They may

say what they will of their orbs in the skies, But this earth is the pla - net for

you, love, and me.

II.

In Mercury's star, where each minute can bring them
New sunshine and wit from the fountain on high,
Tho' the Nymphs may have livelier poets to sing them,
They 've none, even there, more enamour'd than I.
And, as long as this harp can be waken'd to love,
And that eye its divine inspiration shall be,
They may talk as they will of their Edens above,
But this earth is the planet for you, love, and me.

III.

In that star of the west, by whose shadowy splendour,
At twilight so often we 've roam'd through the dew,
There are maidens, perhaps, who have bosoms as tender,
And look, in their twilights, as lovely as you.
But, though they were even more bright than the queen
Of that isle they inhabit in heaven's blue sea,
As I never these fair young celestials have seen,
Why, — this earth is the planet for you, love, and me.

IV.

As for those chilly orbs on the verge of creation,
Where sunshine and smiles must be equally rare,
Did they want a supply of cold hearts for that station,
Heaven knows, we have plenty on earth we could spare.
Oh think what a world we should have of it here,
If the haters of peace, of affection, and glee,
Were to fly up to Saturn's comfortless sphere,
And leave earth to such spirits as you, love, and me.

NE'ER ASK THE HOUR.

AIR—MY HUSBAND'S A JOURNEY TO PORTUGAL GONE.

Ne'er ask the hour—what is it to us How Time deals out his treasures? The gold-en mo-ments, lent us thus, Are not *his* coin, but Pleasure's. If count-ing them o - ver could add to their bliss-es, I 'd num - ber each glo - rious se-cond; But mo-ments of joy are, like Les - bia's kiss - es, Too

quick and sweet to be reck-on'd. Then fill the cup—what is it to us How

Time his cir-cle measures? The fai-ry hours we call up thus, O-

bey no wand but Pleasure's!

II.

Young Joy ne'er thought of counting hours,
 Till Care, one summer's morning,
Set up, among his smiling flowers,
 A dial, by way of warning.
But Joy loved better to gaze on the sun,
 As long as its light was glowing,

Than to watch with old Care how the shadow stole on,
 And how fast that light was going.
So fill the cup — what is it to us
 How Time his circle measures?
The fairy hours we call up thus,
 Obey no wand but Pleasure's!

SAIL ON, SAIL ON.

With mournful defiance.

AIR—THE HUMMING OF THE BAN.

Sail on, sail on, thou fear-less bark— Wher-ev-er blows the wel come wind, It

[can-not lead to scenes more dark, More sad than those we leave be-hind. Each

II.

Sail on, sail on, through endless space,
　　Through calm, through tempest, stop no more.
The stormiest sea's a resting-place
　　To him who leaves such hearts on shore.
Or, if some desert land we meet,
　　Where never yet false-hearted men
Profaned a world, that else were sweet,
　　Then rest thee, bark, but not till then.

THE PARALLEL.

YES, SAD ONE OF ZION! IF CLOSELY RESEMBLING.

Mournfully.

AIR—I WOULD RATHER THAN IRELAND.

Yes, sad one of Si - on!* if close - ly re - sem - bling, In

shame and in sor - row, thy with-er'd - up heart— If drink-ing deep,

* These verses were written after the perusal of a treatise by Mr. Hamilton, professing to prove that the Irish were originally Jews.

deep, of the same "cup of tremb-ling" Could make us thy chil-dren, our

pa-rent thou art.

II.

Like thee doth our nation lie conquer'd and broken,
    And fall'n from her head is the once royal crown;
In her streets, in her halls, Desolation hath spoken,
    And, "while it is day, yet her sun hath gone down."

III.

Like thine doth her exile, mid dreams of returning,
    Die far from the home it were life to behold;
Like thine do her sons, in the day of their mourning,
    Remember the bright things that bless'd them of old!

IV.

Ah, well may we call her, like thee, "the Forsaken,"
    Her boldest are vanquish'd, her proudest are slaves;
And the harps of her minstrels, when gayest they waken,
    Have breathings as sad as the wind over graves!

V.

Yet hadst thou thy vengeance—yet came there the morrow,
    That shines out, at last, on the longest dark night,
When the sceptre, that smote thee with slavery and sorrow,
    Was shiver'd at once, like a reed, in thy sight.

VI.

When that cup, which for others the proud Golden City
    Had brimm'd full of bitterness, drench'd her own lips,
And the world she had trampled on heard, without pity,
    The howl in her halls and the cry from her ships.

VII.

When the curse Heaven keeps for the haughty came over,
    Her merchants rapacious, her rulers unjust,
And—a ruin, at last, for the earth-worm to cover,—
    The Lady of Kingdoms lay low in the dust.

DRINK OF THIS CUP.

AIR—PADDY O'RAFFERTY.

Drink of this cup—you'll find there's a spell in Its ev-e-ry drop 'gainst the

ills of mor-tal-i-ty: Talk of the cor-dial that sparkled for He-len, Her cup was a fic-tion, but

this is re-al-i-ty. Would you for-get the dark world we are in, On-ly taste of the

bub-ble that gleams on the top of it; But would you rise a-bove earth, till a-kin To im-

mor-tals themselves, you must drain ev'-ry drop of it. Send round the cup—for oh! there's a spell in its

ev - e - ry drop 'gainst the ills of mor-tal-i - ty: Talk of the cor-dial that spar-kled for He-len, Her

cup was a fic-tion, but this is re-al-i-ty.

II.

Never was philter form'd with such power
    To charm and bewilder as this we are quaffing;
Its magic began when, in Autumn's rich hour,
    As a harvest of gold in the fields it stood laughing.
There having, by nature's enchantment, been fill'd
    With the balm and the bloom of her kindliest weather,
This wonderful juice from its core was distill'd,
    To enliven such hearts as are here brought together!
Then drink of the cup—you 'll find there 's a spell in
    Its every drop 'gainst the ills of mortality:
Talk of the cordial that sparkled for HELEN,
    Her cup was a fiction, but this is reality.

III.

And though, perhaps—but breathe it to no one—
    Like caldrons the witch brews at midnight so awful,
In secret this philter was first taught to flow on,
    Yet—'t is n't less potent for being unlawful.
What, though it may taste of the smoke of that flame,
    Which in silence extracted its virtue forbidden —
Fill up—there 's a fire in some hearts I could name,
    Which may work too its charm, though now lawless and hidden.
So drink of the cup—for oh there 's a spell in
    Its every drop 'gainst the ills of mortality:
Talk of the cordial that sparkled for HELEN,
    Her cup was a fiction, but this is reality.

OF ALL THE FAIR MONTHS, THAT ROUND THE SUN.

SONG OF O'DONOHUE'S MISTRESS.*

Smoothly and in moderate time.

AIR—THE LITTLE AND GREAT MOUNTAIN.

Of all the fair mounths that round the Sun In light - link'd

dance their cir - cles run, Sweet May, sweet May, shine thou for me, Sweet

* The particulars of the tradition respecting O'Donohue and his White Horse may be found in Mr. Weld's Account of Killarney, or, more fully detailed, in Derrick's Letters. For many years after his death, the spirit of this hero is supposed to have been seen, on the morning of May-day, gliding over the lake on his favourite white horse, to the sound of sweet unearthly music, and preceded by groups of youths and maidens, who flung wreaths of delicate spring-flowers in his path. Among other stories connected with this Legend of the Lakes, it is said that there was a young and beautiful girl, whose imagination was so impressed with the idea of this visionary chieftain, that she fancied herself in love with him, and at last, in a fit of insanity, on a May-morning, threw herself into the Lake.

May, shine thou for me; For still when thy ear-liest beams a-rise, That Youth, who be-neath the blue lake lies, Sweet May, Sweet May, re-turns to me, Sweet May, re-turns to me.

II.

Of all the bright haunts, where daylight leaves,
Its lingering smile on golden eves,
   Fair Lake, fair Lake, thou 'rt dearest to me;
For when the last April sun grows dim,
Thy Naiads prepare his steed for him
   Who dwells, who dwells, bright Lake, in thee

III.

Of all the proud steeds, that ever bore
Young plumed Chiefs on sea or shore,
   White Steed, white Steed, most joy to thee,
Who still, with the first young glance of spring.
From under that glorious lake dost bring
   My love, my love, my chief, to me.

IV.

While, white as the sail some bark unfurls,
When newly launch'd, thy long mane* curls,
   Fair Steed, fair Steed, as white and free;
And spirits, from all thee lake's deep bowers,
Glide o'er the blue wave scattering flowers,
   Fair Steed, around my love and thee.

V.

Of all the sweet deaths that maidens die,
Whose lovers beneath the cold wave lie,
   Most sweet, most sweet, that death will be,
Which, under the next May evening's light,
When thou and thy steed are lost to sight,
   Dear love, dear love, I 'll die for thee.

   * The boatmen at Killarney call those waves which come on a windy day, crested with foam, "O'Donohue's white horses."

ECHO.

HOW SWEET THE ANSWER ECHO MAKES.

II.

Yet Love hath echoes truer far,
    And far more sweet,
Than e'er beneath the moonlight's star,
Of horn, or lute, or soft guitar,
    The songs repeat.

III.

'T is when the sigh, in youth sincere,
    And only then —
The sigh, that 's breathed for one to hear,
Is by that one, that only dear,
    Breathed back again.

OH, BANQUET NOT IN THOSE SHINING BOWERS.

In moderate time, with a careless melancholy.

AIR—PLANXTY IRWINE.

Oh, ban - quet not in those shin - ing bow-ers Where Youth re - sorts—but come to me, For

mine's a gar-den of fad - ed flow-ers, More fit for sor-row, for age, and thee. And

there we shall have our feast of tears, And ma-ny a cup in si - lence pour—Our

guests the shades of for - mer years, Our toasts to lips that bloom no more.

II.

There, while the myrtle's withering boughs
  Their lifeless leaves around us shed,
We 'll brim the bowl to broken vows,
  To friends long lost, the changed, the dead!
Or, as some blighted laurel waves
  Its branches o'er the dreary spot,
We 'll drink to those neglected graves,
  Where Valour sleeps, unnamed, forgot!

SHALL THE HARP THEN BE SILENT?*

AIR—"MACFARLANE'S LAMENTATION."

Shall the Harp then be si - lent, when he, who first gave To our country a name, is with-drawn from all eyes? Shall a

min - strel of E - rin stand mute by the grave, Where the first—where the

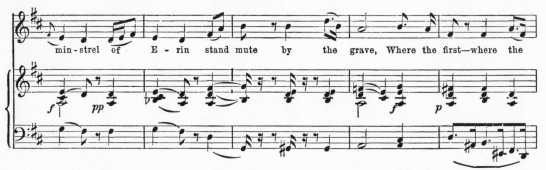

* It is only the two first verses that are either fitted or intended to be sung.

last of her Pa - tri - ots lies?

II.

What a union of all the affections and powers,
By which life is exalted, embellish'd, refined,
Was embraced in that spirit—whose centre was ours,
While its mighty circumference circled mankind!

III.

Oh, who that loves Erin—or who that can see,
Through the waste of her annals, that epoch sub-
lime—
Like a pyramid, raised in the desert—where he
And his glory stand out to the eyes of all time!—

IV.

That *one* lucid interval, snatch'd from the gloom
And the madness of ages, when, fill'd with his
soul,
A Nation o'erleap'd the dark bounds of her doom,
And, for *one* sacred instant, touch'd Liberty's goal!

V.

Who, that ever hath heard him—hath drunk at the source
Of that wonderful eloquence, all Erin's own,
In whose high-thoughted daring the fire, and the force,
And the yet untamed spring of her spirit are shown—

VI.

An eloquence rich—wheresoever its wave
Wander'd free and triumphant—with thoughts that
shone through,
As clear as the brook's "stone of lustre," and gave,
With the flash of the gem, its solidity too!

VII.

Who, that ever approach'd him, when, free from the crowd
In a home full of love, he delighted to tread
'Mong the trees which a nation had given, and which bow'd,
As if each brought a new civic crown for his head—

VIII.

That home, where—like him, who, as fable hath told,*
Put the rays from his brow, that his child might come
near—
Every glory forgot, the most wise of the old
Became all that the simplest and youngest hold dear!

IX.

Is there one, who hath thus, through his orbit of life,
But at distance observed him—through glory, through
blame,
In the calm of retreat, in the grandeur of strife,
Whether shining or clouded, still high and the same—

X.

Such a union of all that enriches life's hour,
Of the sweetness we love and the greatness we praise,
As that type of simplicity blended with power,
A child with a thunderbolt only portrays.—

XI.

Oh no—not a heart, that e'er knew him, but mourns,
Deep, deep o'er the grave, where such glory is
shrined—
O'er a monument Fame will preserve, 'mong the urns
Of the wisest, the bravest, the best of mankind!

* Apollo, in his interview with Phaëton, as described by Ovid: — "*Deposuit radios, propiùsque accedere jussit.*"

THEE, THEE, ONLY THEE!

THE DAWNING OF MORN.

With melancholy expression.

AIR—STACA AN MHARAGA (THE MARKET-STAKE).

The dawning of morn, the day-light's sink-ing, The night's long hours, still find me think-ing Of thee, thee, on-ly thee. When friends are met, and gob-lets crown'd, And smiles are near that

once en-chant-ed, Un-reach'd by all that sun-shine round, My

soul, like some dark spot, is haunt-ed By thee, thee, on-ly thee.

II.

Whatever in fame's high path could waken
My spirit once is now forsaken
    For thee, thee, only thee.
Like shores by which some headlong bark
    To the ocean hurries, resting never,
Life's scenes go by me, bright or dark
    I know not, heed not, hastening ever
        To thee, thee, only thee.

III.

I have not a joy but of thy bringing,
And pain itself seems sweet when springing
    From thee, thee, only thee.
Like spells that nought on earth can break,
    Till lips that know the charm have spoken,
This heart, howe'er the world may wake
    Its grief, its scorn, can but be broken
        By thee, thee, only thee.

REMEMBER THEE!

Not too slow, and with strong feeling.

AIR—CASTLE TIROWEN.

Re - mem - ber thee! yes, while there's life in this

heart It shall nev - er for - get thee, all lorn as thou art; More

dear in thy sor - row, thy gloom, and thy show'rs, Than the rest of the

world in their sun - ni - est hours.

II.

Wert thou all that I wish thee, great, glorious, and free,
First flower of the earth, and first gem of the sea,
I might hail thee with prouder, with happier brow,
But oh! could I love thee moore deeply than now?

III.

No, thy chains as they rankle, thy blood as it runs,
But make thee more painfully dear to thy sons —
Whose hearts, like the young of the desert bird's nest,
Drink love in each life-drop that flows from thy breast.

MY GENTLE HARP ONCE MORE I WAKEN.

With feeling.

AIR—THE COINA OR DIRGE

My gen-tle Harp! once more I wa-ken The sweet-ness of thy slumb'ring

strain; In tears our last fare-well was ta-ken, And now in tears we meet a-

gain. No light of joy hath o'er thee bro-ken, But, like those Harps whose heav'nly

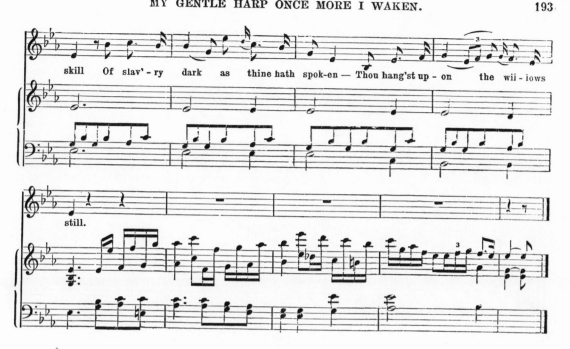

skill Of slav'-ry dark as thine hath spok-en — Thou hang'st up-on the wil-lows still.

II.

And yet, since last thy chord resounded,
  An hour of peace and triumph came,
And many an ardent bosom bounded
  With hopes — that now are turn'd to shame.
Yet even then, while peace was singing
  Her halcyon song o'er land and sea,
Tho' joy and hope to others bringing,
  She only brought new tears to thee.

III.

Then, who can ask for notes of pleasure,
  My drooping Harp, from chords like thine?
Alas, the lark's gay morning measure
  As ill would suit the swan's decline!
Or how shall I, who love, who bless thee,
  Invoke thy breath for Freedom's strains,
When ev'n the wreaths in which I dress thee
  Are sadly mix'd — half flow'rs, half chains.

IV.

But come — if yet thy frame can borrow
  One breath of joy, oh, breathe for me,
And show the world, in chains and sorrow,
  How sweet thy music still can be;
How gaily, ev'n 'mid gloom surrounding,
  Thou yet canst wake at pleasure's thrill —
Like Memnon's broken image sounding,
  'Mid desolation tuneful still.

13

WHENE'ER 1 SEE THOSE SMILING EYES.

AIR—FATHER QUINN.

Slow and tenderly.

When-e'er I see those smil-ing eyes, All fill'd with hope, and joy, and light, As if no cloud could ev-er rise, To dim a heav'n so

pure - ly bright; I sigh to think how soon that brow In grief may lose its

ev' - ry ray, And that light heart, so joy-ous now, Al - most for-get it

once was gay.

II.

For time will come with all its blights,
The ruin'd hope, the friend unkind,
And love, that leaves, where'er it lights,
A chill'd or burning heart behind: —
While youth, that now like snow appears,
Ere sullied by the dark'ning rain,
When once 't is touch'd by sorrow's tears
Will never shine so bright again.

IF THOU'LT BE MINE

Flowing and simple.

AIR—THE WINNOWING SHEET.

If thou'lt be mine, the trea-sures of air, Of earth, and sea shall

lie at thy feet; What-ev-er in Fan-cy's eye looks fair, Or in

espress.

Hope's **sweet** mu - sic sounds most sweet, Shall be ours, if thou wilt be

mine, love!

II.

Bright flowers shall bloom wherever we rove,
A voice divine shall talk in each stream,
The stars shall look like worlds of love,
And this earth be all one beautiful dream
In our eyes—if thou wilt be mine, love!

III.

And thoughts whose source is hidden and high,
Like streams that come from heaven-ward hills.
Shall keep our hearts, like meads that lie
To be bath'd by those eternal rills,
Ever green, if thou wilt be mine, love!

IV.

All this and more the Spirit of Love
Can breathe o'er them who feel his spells;
That heaven which forms his home above,
He can make on earth, wherever he dwells,
As thou 'lt own, if thou wilt be mine, love!

OH FOR THE SWORDS OF FORMER TIME!

In moderate time and with spirit.

AIR—NAME UNKNOWN.

Oh for the swords of for-mer time! Oh for the men who bore them, When,

arm'd for Right, they stood sub-lime, And ty-rants crouch'd be-fore them! When pure yet, ere

courts be-gan With hon-ours to en-slave him, The best hon-ours worn by Man Were

those which Vir-tue gave him. Oh for the swords of for-mer time! Oh for the men who

bore them, When, arm'd for Right, they stood sub-lime, And ty-rants crouch'd be-fore them!

II.

Oh for the Kings who flourish'd then!
Oh for the pomp that crown'd them,
When hearts and hands of freeborn men
Were all the ramparts round them!
When, safe built on bosoms true,
The throne was but the centre,
Round which Love a circle drew,
That Treason durst not enter.
Oh for the Kings who flourish'd then!
Oh for the pomp that crown'd them,
When hearts and hands of freeborn men
Were all the ramparts round them!

DOWN IN THE VALLEY, COME MEET ME TO-NIGHT.

THE FORTUNE-TELLER.

Significantly and in moderate time.

AIR—OPEN THE DOOR SOFTLY.

pp e staccato.

mf pp

smorz.

Down in the val - ley, come,

f *pp*

sempre staccato molto.

meet me to - night, I'll tell you your for - tune tru - ly As ev - er 't was told, by the

new moon's light, To young maid-en, shin-ing as new - ly — As ev-er 't was told, by the

new moon's light, To young maid-en, shin - ing as new - ly.

II.

But, for the world, let no one be nigh,
   Lest haply the stars should deceive me;
Such secrets between you and me and the sky
   Should never go farther, believe me.

III.

If at that hour the heav'ns be not dim,
   My science shall call up before you
A male apparition — the image of him
   Whose destiny 't is to adore you.

IV.

And if to that phantom you 'll be kind,
   So fondly around you he 'll hover,
You 'll hardly, my dear, any difference find
   'Twixt him and a true living lover.

V.

Down at your feet, in the pale moonlight,
   He 'll kneel, with a warmth of devotion —
An ardour, of which such an innocent sprite
   You 'd scarcely believe had a notion.

VI.

What other thoughts and events may arise,
   As in destiny's book I 've not seen them,
Must only be left to the stars and your eyes
   To settle, ere morning, between them.

OH. YE DEAD!

AIR—PLOUGH TUNE.

Oh, ye Dead! oh, ye Dead! whom we know by the light you give From your cold gleam-ing eyes, though you move like men who live— Why leave you thus your graves, In far-off fields and waves, Where the worm and the sea-bird on-ly know your

bed, To haunt this spot, where all Those eyes that wept your

fall, And the hearts that be - wail'd you, like your own, lie

dead?

II.

It is true, it is true, we are shadows cold and wan;
And the fair and the brave whom we lov'd on earth are gone;
But still, thus ev'n in death,
So sweet the living breath
Of the fields and the flow'rs in our youth we wander'd o'er,
That ere, condemn'd, we go
To freeze 'mid Hecla's snow,
We would taste it awhile, and think we live once more!

OH, THE SIGHT ENTRANCING.

AIR—PLANXTY SUDLEY.

Triumphantly.

I. Oh the sight en - tranc - ing, When morn - ing's beam is glanc -

ing O'er files, ar - ray'd With helm and blade, And plumes in the gay wind

danc - ing! When heart's are all high beat - ing, And the trum - pet's voice re-

OH, THE SIGHT ENTRANCING.

tranc - ing, When the morn - ing's beam is glanc - ing O'er files, ar-

ray'd with helm and blade, And plumes in the gay wind danc - ing!

II.

Yet, 't is not helm or feather —
For ask yon despot, whether
    His plumed bands
    Could bring such hands
And hearts as curs together.
Leave pomps to those who need 'em —
Give man but heart and freedom,
    And proud he braves
    The gaudiest slaves
That crawl where monarchs lead 'em.

The sword may pierce the beaver,
Stone walls in time may sever,
    'T is mind alone,
    Worth steel and stone,
That keeps men free for ever.
Oh that sight entrancing,
When the morning's beam is glancing
    O'er files array'd
    With helm and blade,
And in Freedom's cause advancing!

SWEET INNISFALLEN.

Rather slow and feelingly.

AIR—THE CAPTIVATING YOUTH.

Sweet Innisfal-len, fare thee well, May calm and sunshine long be thine! How fair thou art let oth-ers tell, But oh to *feel* how fair be mine!

II.
Sweet Innisfallen, fare thee well,
　And oft may light around thee smile,
As soft as on that ev'ning fell,
　When first I saw thy fairy isle!

III.
Thou wert *too* lovely then for one
　Who had to turn to paths of care —
Who had through vulgar crowds to run,
　And leave thee bright and silent there;

IV.
No more along thy shores to come,
　But, on the world's dim ocean tost,
Dream of thee sometimes, as a home
　Of sunshine he had seen and lost!

V.
Far better in thy weeping hours
　To part from thee, as I do now,
When mist 's o'er thy blooming bowers,
　Like sorrow's veil on beauty's brow.

VI.
For, though unrivall'd still thy grace,
　Thou dost not look, as then, *too* blest,
But, in thy shadows, seem'st a place
　Where weary man might hope to rest —

VII.
Might hope to rest, and find in thee
　A gloom like Eden's, on the day
He left its shade, when every tree,
　Like thine, hung weeping o'er his way!

VIII.
Weeping or smiling, lovely isle!
　And still the lovelier for thy tears —
For though but rare thy sunny smile,
　'T is Heaven's own glance, when it appears.

IX.
Like feeling hearts, whose joys are few,
　But, when *indeed* they come, divine —
The steadiest light the sun e'er threw
　Is lifeless to one gleam of thine!

FROM THIS HOUR THE PLEDGE IS GIVEN.

With spirit and feeling.

AIR—RENARDINE.

From this hour the pledge is giv - en, From this hour my soul is thine: Come what will, from earth or heav - en, Weal or woe, thy fate be mine. When the proud and great stood by thee, None dared thy rights to

spurn, And when now they're false and fly thee, Shall I too base-ly turn? No,—what-

e'er the fires that try thee, In the same this heart shall burn.

rallentando.

colla voce.

II.

Tho' the sea, where thou embarkest,
  Offers now no friendly shore,
Light may come where all looks darkest,
  Hope hath life, when life seems o'er.
And of those past ages dreaming,
  When glory deck'd thy brow,
Oft I fondly think, though seeming
  So fall'n and clouded now,
Thou 'lt again break forth, all beaming, —
None so bright, so blest as thou.

14

'T WAS ONE OF THOSE DREAMS.

With feeling, but not too slow.

AIR—THE SONG OF THE WOODS.

'T was one of those dreams that by

Mu - sic are brought, Like a bright sum - mer haze, o'er the

Po - et's warm thought — When, lost in the fu ture, his
soul wan - ders on, And all of this life, but its
sweet - ness, is gone.

II.

The wild notes he heard o'er the water were those
To which he had sung Erin's bondage and woes,
And the breath of the bugle now wafted them o'er
From Dinis' green isle to Glenä's wooded shore.

III.

He listen'd—while, high o'er the eagle's rude nest,
The lingering sounds on their way loved to rest;
And the echoes sung back from their full mountain quire,
As if loth to let song so enchanting expire.

IV.

It seem'd as if every sweet note, that died here,
Was again brought to life in some airier sphere,
Some heaven in those hills, where the soul of the strain
That had ceased upon earth was awaking again!

V.

Oh forgive, if, while listening to music, whose breath
Seem'd to circle his name with a charm against death,
He should feel a proud Spirit within him proclaim,
"Even so shalt thou live in the echoes of Fame:

VI.

"Even so, though thy memory should now die away,
'T will be caught up again in some happier day,
And the hearts and the voices of Erin prolong,
Through the answering Future, thy name and thy song!"

QUICK! WE HAVE BUT A SECOND.

AIR—PADDY SNAP.

Quick! we have but a se-cond, Fill round the cup, while you may; For Time, the churl, hath beckon'd, And we must a-way — a-way! Grasp the plea-sure that's fly-ing, For oh! not Or-pheus' strain Could keep sweet hours from dy-ing, Or charm them to life a-gain— Then,

quick! we have but a se-cond, Fill round the cup while you may, For Time, the churl, hath

beckon'd, And we must a - way, — a - way!

II.

See the glass, how it flushes,
　Like some young Hebe's lip,
And half meets thine, and blushes
　That thou should'st delay to sip.
Shame, o shame unto thee,
　If ever thou see'st that day,
When a cup or lip shall woo thee,
　And turn untouch'd away!
Then quick! we have but a second,
　Fill round, fill round, while you may,
For Time, the churl, hath beckon'd,
　And we must away,—away!

THE DREAM OF THOSE DAYS.*

Mournfully.

AIR—I LOVE YOU ABOVE ALL THE REST.

The dream of those days when first I sung thee is o'er, Thy tri - umph hath stain'd the charm thy sor - rows then wore, And ev'n of the light which

* Written in one of those moods of hopelessness and disgust which come occasionally over the mind, in contemplating the present state of Irish patriotism.

Hope once shed o'er thy chains, A - las, not a gleam to grace thy

free - dom re - mains.

II.

Say, is it that slavery sunk so deep in thy heart,
That still the dark brand is there, though clainless thou art;
And Freedom's sweet fruit, for which thy spirit long burn'd,
Now, reaching at last thy lip, to ashes hath turn'd.

III.

Up Liberty's steep by Truth and Eloquence led,
With eyes on her temple fix'd, how proud was thy tread!
Ah, better thou ne'er hadst lived that summit to gain,
Or died in the porch, than thus dishonour the fane.

SING, SWEET HARP, OH SING TO ME.

AIR—UNKNOWN.

With mournful expression.

Sing, sweet Harp, oh sing to me Some song of an-cient days, Whose sounds, in this sad me-mo-ry, Long bu-ried dreams shall raise;—

Some lay that tells of van-ish'd fame, Whose light once round us shone; Of

no-ble pride, now turn'd to shame, And hopes for ev- er gone. — Oh sing, sad Harp, thus

sing to me, A- like our doom is cast, Both lost to all but me-mo-ry, We

live but in the past.

II.

How mournfully the midnight air
　Among thy chords doth sigh,
As if it sought some echo there
　Of voices long gone by; —
Of Chieftains, now forgot, who beam'd
　The foremost then in fame;
Of Bards who, once immortal deem'd,
　Now sleep without a name. —
In vain, sad Harp, the midnight air
　Among thy chords doth sigh;
In vain it seeks an echo there
　Of voices long gone by.

III.

Could'st thou but call those spirits round
　Who once, in bower and hall,
Sate list'ning to thy magic sound, —
　Now mute and mould'ring all.
But, no—they would but wake to weep
　Their children's slavery;
Then leave them in their dreamless sleep,
　The Dead, at least, are free. —
Oh! hush, sad Harp, that dreary tone,
　That knell of Freedom's day,
Or, list'ning to its deathlike moan,
　Let me, too, die away.

FAIREST! PUT ON AWHILE.

AIR—CUMMILUM.

In moderate time.

Fair - est! put on a - while These pin - ions of light I bring thee, And o'er thine own green isle In fan - cy let me wing thee.

Nev - er did A - riel's plume, At gold - en sun - set, hov - er O'er such scenes of bloom As

I shall waft thee o - ver!

II.

Fields, where the spring delays,
   And fearlessly meets the ardour
Of the warm Summer's gaze,
   With only her tears to guard her.
Rocks, through myrtle boughs
   In grace majestic frowning;
Like some bold warrior's brows
   That Love hath just been crowning.

III.

Islets, so freshly fair,
   That never hath bird come nigh them,
But from his course thro' air
   He hath been won down by them. —
Types, sweet maid, of thee,
   Whose look, whose blush inviting,
Never did Love yet see
   From heav'n, without alighting.

IV.

Lakes, where the pearl lies hid,
   And caves, where the gem is sleeping,]
Bright as the tears thy lid
   Lets fall in lonely weeping.
Glens, where Ocean comes,
   To 'scape the wild wind's rancour,
And harbours, worthiest homes
   Where Freedom's fleet can anchor.

V.

Then, if, while scenes so grand,
   So beautiful, shine before thee,
Pride for thy own dear land
   Should haply be stealing o'er thee,
Oh, let grief come first,
   O'er pride itself victorious —
Thinking how man hath curst
   What Heaven had made so glorious.

AND DOTH NOT A MEETING LIKE THIS.

In moderate time and with feeling.

AIR—UNKNOWN.

And doth not a meet - ing like this make a - mends For all the long years I've been

wand-'ring a-way— To see thus a-round me my youth's ear-ly friends, As

smil-ing and kind as in that hap-py day! Though hap-ly o'er some of your

brows, as o'er mine, The snow-fall of Time may be steal-ing— what then? Like

Alps in the sun-set, thus light-ed by wine, We'll wear the gay tinge of Youth's

AND DOTH NOT A MEETING LIKE THIS.

ros - es a - gain.

II.

What soften'd remembrances come o'er the heart,
  In gazing on those we 've been lost to so long!
The sorrows, the joys, of which once they were part,
  Still round them, like visions of yesterday, throng.
As letters some hand hath invisibly trac'd,
  When held to the flame will steal out on the sight,
So many a feeling, that long seem'd effac'd,
  The warmth of a moment like this brings to light.

III.

And thus, as in memory's bark, we shall glide
  To visit the scenes of our boyhood anew,
Tho' oft we may see, looking down on the tide,
  The wreck of full many a hope shining through;
Yet still, as in fancy we point to the flowers
  That once made a garden of all the gay shore,
Deceiv'd for a moment, we 'll think them still ours,
  And breathe the fresh air of life's morning once more.

IV.

So brief our existence, a glimpse, at the most,
  Is all we can have of the few we hold dear;
And oft even joy is unheeded and lost,
  For want of some heart, that could echo it, near.
Ah, well may we hope, when this short life is gone,
  To meet in some world of more permanent bliss;
For a smile, or a grasp of the hand, hastening on,
  Is all we enjoy of each other in this.

V.

But, come, the more rare such delights to the heart,
  The more we should welcome and bless them the more.
They 're ours, when we meet,—they are lost when we part,
  Like birds that bring summer and fly when 't is o'er.
Thus circling the cup, hand in hand, ere we drink,
  Let Sympathy pledge us, thro' pleasure, thro' pain,
That, fast as a feeling but touches one link,
  Her magic shall send it direct thro' the chain.

SING—SING—MUSIC WAS GIVEN.

Flowingly.

AIR—THE HUMOURS OF BALLAMAGUIRY; OR, THE OLD LANGOLEE.

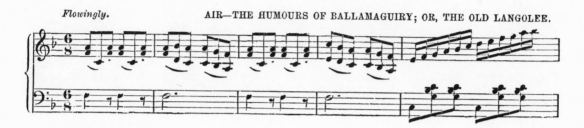

Sing — sing —

Mu - sic was giv - en, To brighten the gay, and kin - dle the lov - ing; Souls here, like

plan - ets in Hea - ven, By har - mo - ny's laws a - lone are kept mov - ing. Beau - ty may

boast of her eyes and her cheeks, But Love from the lips his true ar - che - ry wings; And

she who but feathers the dart, when she speaks, At once sends it home to the heart when she sings. Then

sing — sing — Mu - sic was giv - en, To brighten the gay, and kin - dle the lov - ing;

Souls here, like plan-ets in Heav-en, By har - mo - ny's laws a - lone are kept mov - ing.

II.

When Love, rock'd by his mother,
   Lay sleeping, as calm as slumber could make him,
"Hush, hush," said Venus, "no other
   "Sweet voice but his own is worthy to wake him."
Dreaming of music he slumber'd the while,
   Till faint from his lip a soft melody broke,
And Venus, enchanted, look'd on with a smile,
   While Love to his own sweet singing awoke.
   Then sing—sing—Music was given
     To brighten the gay, and kindle the loving;
   Souls here, like planets in heaven,
     By harmony's laws alone are kept moving.

15

THE MOUNTAIN SPRITE.

IN YONDER VALLEY THERE DWELT, ALONE.

In moderate time and playfully.

AIR—THE MOUNTAIN SPRITE.

In yon-der val - ley there dwelt, a - lone   A   youth, whose life   all   had

calm-ly flown,   Till   spells came o'er   him, and,   day and night,   He was

haunted and watch'd by a Mountain Sprite, He was haunt-ed and watch'd by a

Mountain Sprite.

II.

As once, by moonlight, he wander'd o'er
The golden sands of that island shore,
A foot-print sparkled before his sight —
'T was the fairy foot of the Mountain Sprite!

III.

Beside a fountain, one sunny day,
As bending over the stream he lay,
There peep'd down o'er him two eyes of light,
And he saw in that mirror, the Mountain Sprite.

IV.

He turn'd — but, lo, like a startled bird,
That spirit fled — and the youth but heard
Sweet music, such as marks the flight
Of some bird of song, from the Mountain Sprite

V.

One night, still haunted by that bright look,
The boy, bewilder'd, his pencil took,
And, guided only by memory's light,
Drew the once-seen form of the Mountain Sprite.

VI.

"Oh thou, who lovest the shadow," cried
A voice, low whisp'ring by his side,
"Now turn and see," — here the youth's delight
Seal'd the rosy lips of the Mountain Sprite.

VII.

"Of all the Spirits of land and sea,"
Then rapt he murmur'd, "there's none like thee,
"And oft, oh oft, may thy foot thus light
"In this lonely bower, sweet Mountain Sprite!"

AS VANQUISH'D ERIN

With expression.

AIR—THE BOYNE WATER.

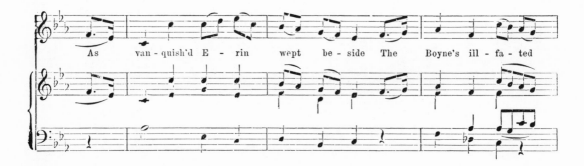

As van-quish'd E-rin wept be-side The Boyne's ill-fa-ted

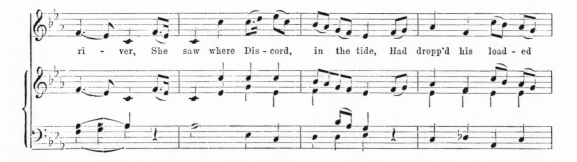

ri-ver, She saw where Dis-cord, in the tide, Had dropp'd his load-ed

qui-ver. "Lie hid," she cried, "ye ve-nom'd darts, Where mor-tal eye may

shun   you,—Lie   hid—for   oh!   the   stain of hearts That   bled   for   me   is

on   you."

II.

But vain her wish, her weeping vain, —
 As Time too well hath taught her —
Each year the Fiend returns again,
 And dives into that water;
And brings, triumphant, from beneath
 His shafts of desolation,
And sends them, wing'd with worse than death,
 Through all her madd'ning nation.

III.

Alas for her who sits and mourns,
 Ev'n now, beside that river —
Unwearied still the Fiend returns,
 And stor'd is still his quiver.
"When will this end, ye Powers of Good?"
 She weeping asks for ever;
But only hears, from out that flood,
 The Demon answer, "Never!"

DESMOND'S SONG.*

BY THE FEAL'S WAVE BENIGHTED.

AIR—UNKNOWN.†

By the Feal's wave be-night-ed, Not a star in the skies, To thy door by Love light-ed, I first saw those eyes. Some

* "Thomas, the heir of the Desmond family, had accidentally been so engaged in the chase, that he was benighted near Tralee, and obliged to take shelter at the Abbey of Feal, in the house of one of his dependents, called Mac Cormac. Catherine, a beautiful daughter of his host, instantly inspired the Earl with a violent passion, which he could not subdue. He married her, and by this inferior alliance alienated his followers, whose brutal pride regarded this indulgence of his love as an unpardonable degradation of his family." — LELAND, vol. ii.

† The Air has been already so successfully supplied with words by Mr. Bayly, that I should have left it untouched, if we could have spared so interesting a melody out of our collection.

voice whis-per'd o'er me, As thy thresh-old I crost, There was

ru-in be-fore me, If I loved, I was lost.

espress.

slentando. *mf* *p*

II.

Love came, and brought sorrow
  Too soon in his train;
Yet so sweet, that to-morrow
  'T were welcome again.
Though misery's full measure
  My portion should be,
I would drain it with pleasure,
  If pour'd out by thee.

III.

You, who call it dishonour
  To bow to this flame,
If you 've eyes, look but on her,
  And blush while you blame.
Hath the pearl less whiteness
  Because of its birth?
Hath the violet less brightness
  For growing near earth?

IV.

No—Man for his glory
  To ancestry flies;
But Woman's bright story
  Is told in her eyes.
While the Monarch but traces
  Thro' mortals his line,
Beauty, born of the Graces,
  Ranks next to Divine!

THEY KNOW NOT MY HEART.

AIR—COOLON DAS.

They know not my heart, who be - lieve there can

be One stain of this earth in its feel - ings for thee; Who think, while I

see thee in beau-ty's young hour, As pure as the morn-ing's first dew on the

flow'r, I could harm what I love — as the Sun's wan-ton ray But

smiles on the dew-drop to waste it a-way!

II.

No—beaming with light as those young features are,
There 's a light round thy heart which is lovelier far
It *is* not that cheek—'t is the soul dawning clear
Thro' its innocent blush makes thy beauty so dear;
As the sky we look up to, though glorious and fair,
Is look'd up to the more, because heaven lies there!

I WISH I WAS BY THAT DIM LAKE.

Mournful.

AIR—I WISH I WAS ON YONDER HILL.

legati.

pp

I wish I was by that dim Lake, Where sin - ful souls their fare - well

take Of this vain world, and half - way lie In death's cold sha - dow,

ere they die. There, there, far from thee, De - ceit - ful world, my home should be— Where,

come what might of gloom and pain, False hope should ne'er de - ceive a - gain!

II.

The lifeless sky, the mournful sound
Of unseen waters, falling round—
The dry leaves quiv'ring o'er my head,
Like man, unquiet ev'n when dead —
These, ay, these should wean
My soul from life's deluding scene,
And turn each thought, each wish I have,
Like willows, downward tow'rds the grave.

III.

As they, who to their couch at night
Would welcome sleep, first quench the light,
So must the hopes, that keep this breast
Awake, be quench'd, ere it can rest.
Cold, cold, my heart must grow,
Unchanged by either joy or woe,
Like freezing founts, where all that's thrown
Within their current turns to stone.

SHE SUNG OF LOVE.

With expression.

AIR—THE MUNSTER MAN.

She sung of Love — while o'er her lyre The ro - sy rays of ev'n - ing

fell, As if to feed with their soft fire The soul with-

in that trem - bling shell. The same rich light hung o'er her

cheek, And play'd a - round those lips, that sung, And spoke as

flowers would sing and speak, If Love could lend their leaves a tongue.

II.

But soon the West no longer burn'd,
   Each rosy ray from heav'n withdrew;
And when to gaze again I turn'd,
   The minstrel's form seem'd fading too.
As if *her* light and heaven's were one,
   The glory all had left that frame;
And from her glimmering lips the tone,
   As from a parting spirit, came.

III.

Who ever lov'd, but had the thought
   That he and all he lov'd must part?
Fill'd with this fear, I flew and caught
   The fading image to my heart —
And cried, "Oh Love! is this thy doom?
   "Oh light of youth's resplendent day!
Must ye then lose your golden bloom,
   "And thus, like sunshine, die away?"

THOUGH HUMBLE THE BANQUET.

In moderate time and with spirit.

AIR—FAREWELL, EAMON.

Though hum-ble the ban-quet to which I in-vite thee, Thou'lt find there the best a poor bard can com-mand: Eyes, beam-ing with wel-come, shall throng round to light thee, And Love serve the

feast with his own will-ing hand.

II.

And though Fortune may seem to have turn'd from the dwelling
    Of him thou regardest her favouring ray,
Thou wilt find there a gift, all her treasures excelling,
    Which, proudly he feels, hath ennobled his way.

III.

'T is that freedom of mind which no vulgar dominion
    Can turn from the path a pure conscience approves;
Which, with hope in the heart, and no chain on the pinion,
    Holds upwards its course to the light which it loves.

IV.

'T is this makes the pride of his humble retreat,
    And, with this, though of all other treasures bereav'd,
The breeze of his garden to him is more sweet
    Than the costliest incense that Pomp e'er receiv'd.

V.

Then, come,—if a board so untempting hath power
    To win thee from grandeur, its best shall be thine;
And there 's one, long the light of the bard's happy bower,
    Who, smiling, will blend her bright welcome with mine.

SONG OF THE BATTLE-EVE.

TO-MORROW, COMRADE, WE.

With martial and melancholy spirit, not too slow.　　　　　　　　AIR—CRUISKEEN LAWN.

* There is, in this single note, a deviation from the original setting of the Air.

quaff, ere we go, boy, go — We 'll take an-o-ther quaff, ere we go.

II.

'T is true, in manliest eyes
A passing tear will rise,
  When we think of the friends we leave lone;
But what can wailing do?
See, our goblet 's weeping too!
  With its tears we 'll chase away our own, boy, our own;
  With its tears we 'll chase away our own.

III.

But daylight 's stealing on; —
The last that o'er us shone
  Saw our children around us play;
The next—ah! where shall we
And those rosy urchins be?
  But—no matter—grasp thy sword and away, boy, away;
  No matter—grasp thy sword and away!

IV.

Let those who brook the chain
Of Saxon or of Dane
  Ignobly by their fire-sides stay;
One sigh to home be given,
One heartfelt prayer to heaven,
  Then, for Erin and her cause, boy, hurra! hurra! hurra!
  Then, for Erin and her cause, hurra!

16

THE WANDERING BARD.

WHAT LIFE LIKE THAT OF THE BARD CAN BE.

With vivacity and expression.

AIR—PLANXTY O'REILLY.

What life like that of the Bard can be, — The wand'ring Bard, who

roams as free   As the mounting lark that o'er him sings, And, like that lark, a mu-sic brings With-

in him, wher-e'er he comes or goes, — A fount that for ev-er flows! The world's to him like

some bright ground, Where fai - ries dance their moonlight round;—If dimm'd the turf where late they trod, The elves but seek some green-er sod; So, when less bright his scene of glee, To an-o-ther a-way flies he!

cresc. mf f p f

II.

Oh, what would have been young Beauty's doom,
Without a bard to fix her bloom?
They tell us, in the moon's bright round,
Things lost in this dark world are found;
So charms, on earth long pass'd and gone,
In the poet's lay live on.—
Would ye have smiles that ne'er grow dim?
You 've only to give them all to him,
Who, with but a touch of Fancy's wand,
Can lend them life, this life beyond,
And fix them high, in Poesy's sky,—
Young stars that never die.

III.

Then, welcome the bard where'er he comes,
For, though he hath countless airy homes,
To which his wing excursive roves,
Yet still, from time to time he loves
To light upon earth and find such cheer
As brightens our banquet here.
No matter how far, how fleet he flies,
You 've only to light up kind young eyes,
Such signal-fires as here are giv'n,—
And down he 'll drop from Fancy's heaven,
The minute such call to love or mirth
Proclaims he 's wanting on earth.

ALONE IN CROWDS TO WANDER ON.

Mournfully.

AIR—SHULE AROON.

A - lone in crowds to wan - der on, And feel that all the charm is gone Which voi - ces dear and eyes be - loved Shed round us once, wher - e'er we roved, This — this the

doom must be Of all who 've loved, and lived to see The few bright things they

thought would stay For ev - er near them, die a - way.

II.

Tho' fairer forms around us throng,
Their smiles to others all belong,
And want that charm which dwells alone
Round those the fond heart calls its own.
Where, where the sunny brow?
The long-known voice—where are they now?
Thus ask I still, nor ask in vain,
The silence answers all too plain.

III.

Oh what is Fancy's magic worth,
If all her heart cannot call forth
One bliss like those we felt of old
From lips now mute, and eyes now cold!
No, no,—her spell is vain,—
As soon could she bring back again
Those eyes themselves from out the grave,
As wake again one bliss they gave.

I'VE A SECRET TO TELL THEE.

In moderate time, and with smoothness.

AIR—OH SOUTHERN BREEZE.

I've a se - cret to tell thee, but, hush! not here, Oh! not where the world its vi - gil keeps: I'll seek, to whisper it in thine ear, Some shore where the Spi - rit of Si - lence sleeps; Where sum-mer's wave un-

mur-m'ring dies, Nor fay can hear the foun-tain's gush; Where, if one note her

night-bird sighs, The Rose saith, chiding him, "Hush, sweet, hush!"

rallentando.

II.

There, 'mid the deep silence of that hour
    When stars can be heard in ocean dip,
Thyself shall, under some rosy bower,
    Sit mute, with thy finger on thy lip:
Like him, the boy, who born among
    The flowers that on the Nile-stream blush,
Sits ever thus, — his only song
    To earth and heaven, "Hush, all, hush!"

SONG OF INNISFAIL.

THEY CAME FROM A LAND BEYOND THE SEA.

In moderate time, and flowingly.

AIR—PEGGY BAWN

They came from a land be-yond the sea, And now o'er the west-ern main, Set sail, in their good ships, gal-lant-ly, From the sun-ny land of Spain. "Oh, where's the Isle we've

seen in dreams, Our des - tin'd home or grave?" —* Thus

sung they, as by the morning's beams They boom'd o'er th'At-lan - tic wave.

II.

And, lo, where afar o'er ocean shines
   A sparkle of radiant green,
As though in that deep lay emerald mines,
   Whose light thro' the wave was seen.
"'T is Innisfail † — 't is Innisfail !"
   Rings o'er the echoing sea,
While, bending to heav'n, the warriors hail
   That home of the brave and free.

III.

Then turn'd they unto the Eastern wave,
   Where now their Day-God's eye
A look of such sunny omen gave
   As lighted up sea and sky.
Nor frown was seen through sky or sea,
   Nor tear o'er leaf or sod,
When first on their Isle of Destiny
   Our great forefathers trod.

* Milesius remembered the remarkable prediction of the principal Druid, who foretold that the posterity of Gadelus should obtain the possession of a Western Island (which was Ireland), and there inhabit."—*Keating.*
† The Island of Destiny, one of the ancient names of Ireland.

THE NIGHT-DANCE.

STRIKE THE GAY HARP! SEE THE MOON IS ON HIGH.

With liveliness and spirit.   AIR—THE NIGHTCAP.

Strike the gay harp! see the moon is on high, And, as true to her beam as the

tides of the ocean, Young hearts, when they feel the soft light of her eye, O - bey the mute call and

heave in - to mo-tion. Then, sound notes—the gay - est, the light-est, That ev - er took wing when

* It is right to mention that the Air is, in this and the seven following bars, transferred to the accompaniment and symphony, being too high for the voice.

heav'n look'd brightest! A - gain! A-gain!

Oh! could such heartstirring mu-sic be heard In that Ci - ty of Statues de-scribed by romancers, So

wakening its spell, ev - en stone would be stirr'd, And sta-tues themselves all start in-to danc-ers!

II.

Why then delay, with such sounds in our ears,
   And the flower of Beauty's own garden before us, —
While stars overhead leave the song of their spheres,
   And, list'ning to ours, hang wondering o'er us?
Again, that strain! — to hear it thus sounding
   Might set even Death's cold pulses bounding —
      Again! Again!
Oh, what delight when the youthful and gay,
   Each with eye like a sunbeam and foot like a feather,
Thus dance, like the hours to the music of May,
   And mingle sweet song and sunshine together!

OH! ARRANMORE, LOVED ARRANMORE.

Moderately slow, and with expression.

AIR—KILLDROUGHALT FAIR.

Oh! Ar - ran-more, loved Ar - ran-more, How oft I dream of thee, And of those days when, by thy shore, I wander'd young and free. Full ma-ny a path I've tried, since then, Through pleasure's flow'r-y maze, But ne'er could find the bliss a-gain I

II.

How blithe upon thy breezy cliffs
    At sunny morn I've stood,
With heart as bounding as the skiffs
    That danc'd along thy flood;
Or, when the western wave grew bright
    With daylight's parting wing,
Have sought that Eden in its light
    Which dreaming poets sing; * —

III.

That Eden, where th' immortal brave
    Dwell in a land serene, —
Whose bowers beyond the shining wave,
    At sunset, oft are seen.
Ah dream too full of sadd'ning truth!
    Those mansions o'er the main
Are like the hopes I built in youth, —
    As sunny and as vain!

* "The inhabitants of Arranmore are still persuaded that, in a clear day, they can see from this coast Hy Brysail or the Enchanted Island, the Paradise of the Pagan Irish, and concerning which they relate a number of romantic stories." — *Beaufort's Ancient Topography of Ireland.*

THERE ARE SOUNDS OF MIRTH.

With liveliness and spirit, but not too fast.

AIR—THE PRIEST IN HIS BOOTS.

There are sounds of mirth in the night air ring-ing, And lamps from ev-e-ry casement shown, While voic-es blithe with-in are sing-ing, That seem to say "Come," in ev-e-ry tone. Ah!

once how light, in Life's young sea-son, My heart had bounded at that sweet lay; Nor

paused to ask of grey-beard Rea-son If I should the si-ren call o-bey.

II.

And see—the lamps still livelier glitter,
  The siren lips more fondly sound;
No, seek, ye nymphs, some victim fitter
  To sink in your rosy bondage bound.
Shall a bard whom not the world in arms
  Could bend to tyranny's rude control,
Thus quail at sight of woman's charms,
  And yield to a smile his freeborn soul?

III.

Thus sung the sage, while, slyly stealing,
  The nymphs their fetters around him cast,
And,—their laughing eyes, the while, concealing,—
  Led Freedom's Bard their slave at last.
For the Poet's heart, still prone to loving,
  Was like that rock of the Druid race,
Which the gentlest touch at once set moving,
  But all earth's power could n't cast from its base.

YOU REMEMBER ELLEN.*

Simply and in moderate time.

AIR—WERE I A CLERK.

You re - mem-ber El - len, our hamlet's pride, How meek-ly she bless'd her hum-ble lot, When the stranger, Wil - liam, had made her his bride, And Love was the light of their low - ly cot. To - ge - ther they toil'd thro' winds and rains, Till Wil-liam at length, in

* This ballad was suggested by a well-known and interesting story, told of a certain Noble Family in England.

sad-ness, said, "We must seek our for-tune on o - ther plains;" — Then, sigh - ing, she left her

low - ly shed.

II.

They roam'd a long and a weary way,
  Nor much was the maiden's heart at ease,
When now, at close of one stormy day,
  They see a proud castle among the trees.
"To-night," said the youth, "we 'll shelter there;
  "The wind blows cold, the hour is late:"
So he blew the horn with a chieftain's air,
  And the Porter bow'd as they pass'd the gate.

III.

"Now, welcome, Lady!" exclaim'd the youth,
  "This castle is thine, and these dark woods all!"
She believ'd him craz'd, but his words were truth,
  For Ellen is Lady of Rosna Hall!
And dearly the Lord of Rosna loves
  What William the stranger woo'd and wed;
And the light of bliss, in these lordly groves,
  Shines pure as it did in the lowly shed.

THE WINE-CUP IS CIRCLING.

AIR—MICHAEL HOY.

In march time, and with spirit.

The wine-cup is cir-cling in Almhin's hall,* And its Chief, 'mid his he-roes re-clin-ing, Looks up, with a sigh, to the trophied wall, Where his fal-chion hangs id-ly shin - ing. When, hark! that shout From the vale with-out;" Arm ye

* The Palace of Finn Mac-Cumhal (the Fingal of Macpherson) in Leinster. It was built on the top of the hill, which has retained from thence the name of the Hill of Allen, in the County of Kildare. The Finians, or Fenii, were the celebrated National Militia of Ireland, which this Chief commanded. The introduction of the Danes in the above song is an anachronism common to most of the Finian and Ossianic legends.

quick, the Dane, the Dane is nigh!" Ev'-ry Chief starts up From his foam-ing cup, And "To bat - tle, on to bat - tle!" is the Fin - ian's cry.

II.

The minstrels have seiz'd their harps of gold,
  And they sing such thrilling numbers,—
'T is like the voice of the Brave, of old,
  Breaking forth from their place of slumbers!
     Spear to buckler rang
     As the minstrels sang,
And the Sun-burst o'er them floated wide;
     While rememb'ring the yoke
     Which their fathers broke,
"On for liberty, for liberty!" the Finians cried.

III.

Like clouds of the night the Northmen came,
  O'er the valley of Almhin lowering;
While onward mov'd, in the light of its fame,
  That banner of Erin, towering.
     With the mingling shock
     Rung cliff and rock,
While, rank on rank, the invaders die:
     And the shout that last
     O'er the dying pass'd
Was "Victory! victory!"—the Finian's cry.

SILENCE IS IN OUR FESTAL HALLS.

AIR—THE GREEN WOODS OF TRUIGHA.

With melancholy feeling.

Si - lence is in our fes - tal halls,* Oh! Son of Song, thy course is o'er; In vain on thee sad E - rin calls, Her minstrel's voice re - sponds no more:— All si - lent as th' E-o-lian

* It is hardly necessary, perhaps, to inform the reader that these lines are meant as a tribute of sincere friendship to the memory of an old and valued colleague in this work, Sir John Stevenson.